ONE
CIRCLE

Tapping the Power of Those Who Know You Best

The

Essential

Guide to

Creating Your

Personal

Advisory Board

MAUREEN FITZGERALD, PH.D.

author of *Mission Possible*

Praise for *One Circle*

"*One Circle* tells you everything you need to know about starting and continuing a circle group. Written in easy-to-understand language and interspersed with dynamic "real life" quotes, ... this book will introduce you to the culture of circles – for professional development or personal growth. I recommend it to anyone who has ever had an interest in circles."

— Beverly Engel, author of *Women Circling the Earth*

"This book can be used by every corporation, every networking group and every mastermind or peer-mentoring group. It is a simple process designed to make any group resilient, effective and meaningful."

— Danna Murray, development consultant and program director, Minerva Foundation

"*One Circle* is a great addition to the books on how the circle process can create and sustain mutually supportive groups ... Fitzgerald's chapters are full of practical advice that might change your life!"

— Christina Baldwin, author, *Calling the Circle* and *Storycatcher*

"Learning how to provide and receive support through a circle of confidants is fundamental to success. This book will help anyone wanting to discover the power and enjoyment of an effective circle of advisors."

— Sue Paish, QC, partner, Fasken Martineau DuMoulin

"If you are unsure of how the power of connectivity and a circle of influence can change your life – you'll need to get this book now!"
—Elaine Allison, author, *The Velvet Hammer*

"Listening is the huge gift of the circle. Fitzgerald's strength is taking something complex and creating a simple yet powerful tool to help people move their lives forward. Enjoy the amazing adventure these well-crafted words invite you to!"
—Elaine Froese, family business coach and author of *Planting the Seed of Hope*

"*One Circle* is an easy-to-use tool that ensures that real conversations happen. A group that adopts this process will gain from the synergy created."
—Shauna Harper, president, Color the Universe Inc.

"Fitzgerald has identified a simple step-by-step process guaranteed to help any group grow and succeed. On a personal note, it was very fulfilling."
—Shelley Leonhardt, executive business coach

"At last a book that helps entrepreneurs and professionals create a community of like-minded people, with clear, engaging and detailed guidance. *One Circle* gives everyone opportunities to develop and sustain meaningful connections for life."
—Karen McGregor, M.Ed., author of *The Inner Entrepreneur*

ONE
CIRCLE

Also by the author

Corporate Circles–Transforming Conflict and Building Trusting Teams. Quinn, 2006.

Hiring, Managing and Keeping the Best–The Complete Canadian Guide for Employers, with Monica Beauregard. McGraw-Hill, 2000.

Mission Possible– Creating a Mission for Work and Life. Quinn, 2003

So You Think You Need a Lawyer–How to Screen, Hire, Manage or Fire a Lawyer. McGraw-Hill, 1998.

Legal Problem Solving–Reasoning, Research and Writing (3rd). Lexis/Nexis, 2005.

ONE CIRCLE

Tapping the Power of Those
Who Know You Best

The Essential
Guide to
Creating a
Personal
Advisory Board

MAUREEN F. FITZGERALD, PhD

Quinn Publishing
Vancouver, BC
Canada

Quinn Publishing
An imprint of CenterPoint Conflict and Collaboration Inc.
PO Box 72030
Vancouver, BC
Canada   V6R 4P2
www.CenterPointInc.com

LIBRARY AND ARCHIVES CANADA CATALOGUING IN PUBLICATION

Fitzgerald, Maureen F.
   One Circle: Tapping the power of those who know you best: The
essential guide to creating a personal advisory board / Maureen F.
Fitzgerald.
Includes bibliographical references.
ISBN 0-9732451-1-5
   1. Social Networks. 2. Mentoring. 3. Self-help groups. I. Title.

HM741.F58 2006 158'.3 2006-901065-X

Layout and design: Joy Woodsworth
Cover design: Lee Edward Födi
Author photo: Reine Mihtla
Editing and proofreading: Naomi Pauls, Paper Trail Publishing

Printed in Canada.

To Jennifer Leslie – JL,
a friend who has always been part of my Circle

Never doubt that a small group of thoughtful, committed citizens can change the world. Indeed, it is the only thing that ever has.

— Margaret Mead

We ourselves feel that what we are doing is just a drop in the ocean. But if that drop was not in the ocean, I think the ocean would be less because of that missing drop.

— Mother Teresa

Contents

Acknowledgments

So many people supported me in writing this book, and so many support me on this journey of life. I am never sure how to thank them all. I want to particularly acknowledge Paul Quinn, Monica Beauregard, Jennifer Leslie, Shauna Harper, Catherine Worrall, Joanne McKinnon, Shelley Leonhardt, Sue Paish, Roslyn Kunin, Bev Voice, Erica Trimble, Diane Ross, Danna Murray, Wendy Zak, Anne Stone, Roxanne Davies, Elaine Froese, Lee Födi, Angela Clarke, Catharine Fennell, Lana Casavant, Mary-Jean Payeur, Kay Pranis, Elaine Decker and, of course, Christina Baldwin.

I would like to acknowledge the following books that most influenced my work:

Calling the Circle, by Christina Baldwin

Peacemaking Circles, by Kay Pranis, Barry Stuart and Mark Wedge

Sacred Circles, by Robin Carnes and Sally Craig

The Way of Council, by Jack M. Zimmerman and Virginia Coyle

Wisdom Circles, by Charles Garfield, Cindy Spring and Sedonia Cahill

Women Circling the Earth, by Beverly Engel

·················

Preface

The circle process is a gentle invitation to change one's relationship to oneself, to the community, and to the wider universe. It offers an awakening of connection and purpose beyond the myriad of differences that keep people apart and in conflict with one another.

— Carolyn Boyes-Watson

You cannot possibly achieve all you want in your life on your own. Nor should you want to. But by simply gathering together a small group, you can truly change the world and also solve your most basic day-to-day problems. Cecile Andrews, in her book *The Circle of Simplicity,* explains that circles are particularly important now because they are meeting so many fundamental unmet human needs, such as:

> the need to find your unique path, the need to feel part of a community, the need to be connected to the universe. In study circles you fulfill the human needs to feel connected – to feel valued, to feel accepted, to be appreciated for your authentic self, to feel that you are free to say what you want without fear of being judged, to talk with people who

share your values, to talk about matters of importance and substance, to feel you are learning how to feel fully alive.[1]

This reflects the modern literature on societal trends and my own experiences.

My story

Several years ago I began searching for a networking group of my own. I decided to join a few mastermind and networking groups to build my law practice and conflict resolution business. Over time I became increasingly frustrated by their processes. None of these groups allowed enough time to get to know the other members, nor did the conversations go to the level necessary to get to the real issues. I felt that these brief conversations were somewhat superficial.

In my frustration, I decided to create my own networking group. In the process I read hundreds of books, articles and websites on various group and networking processes. These included mastermind groups, dream teams, peer-mentoring groups and circles. I discovered Wisdom Circles, Spirit Circles and Council Circles, to name a few, and I learned about the ancient wisdom of circles. I decided to combine what I learned with what I knew about Corporate Circles (for resolving conflict) to create a new model: One Circle.

At the same time, I was speaking regularly to corporations and associations. I was hearing from audiences that there was a real desire for a deeper sense of connectedness and community. Many people were beginning to lose interest in their loose-knit networking groups and book clubs and were finding that their community ties were strained. A growing body of people seem to be seeking ways to create trusting relationships and establish mechanisms for coming together to build community.

Over time, I have seen Circles not only solve problems and help people continuously learn, but also cause people to change deeply held perspectives. When people speak in Circles they transform their individual perspectives and create a new understanding – simply by sharing experiences.

Those who have experienced Circles know how it feels to be able to talk about things that are important and difficult. They know how it feels to find that one contact that made all the difference – that might have taken years to locate on their own. They know what it is like to feel supported in a highly competitive world.

What you will get out of this book

In this book you will learn how to create your own Circle and how to keep it on track and resilient. By being a part of a Circle you will

- create solutions and solve problems

- gain wise advice and information

- generate contacts and resources

- develop skills and continuously learn

- achieve goals and balance

- obtain support and connection

Whom this book is for

Although *One Circle* was written for busy professionals who want to live more focused and balanced lives, this book is useful for anyone and specifically for the following:

> *Entrepreneurs* who want to build their businesses, attract clients and run their businesses more effectively and efficiently.

> *Executives and business owners* who want to be more effective and efficient, excel in their leadership capacity and leave a legacy.

> *Managers* who want to bring together people inside a corporation for purposes of mentoring, professional development and succession planning.

> *Professional women* who want support and advice in achieving their personal and professional goals while living more balanced lives.

> *Parents* who want to share parenting experiences (good and bad) and learn how to cope with, care for and relate to teenagers and aging parents.

> *Career changers* who need contacts, advice and guidance in finding a career that best suits their skills and interests.

Most people recognize that they can be more successful with the help of others, yet many find it difficult to connect with others who will consistently challenge and support them. Those who benefit most from the synergy of a Circle are those who feel somewhat alone or those who have only a few people in whom to confide.

Where to from here?

If you are interested in joining or setting up a Circle, simply read on. You can either take the principles set out here and apply them to your current group or set up your own Circle. Pick a location, select a time, pull together a few people, and begin the conversation! It's that easy.

We cannot solve our problems with the same thinking we used when we created them.

—Albert Einstein

The circle is a spiritual practice with very practical application in the world . . . Circles work well in health-care organizations, in the nonprofit sector, in government and corporate settings – wherever there is a need to allow the hard-earned wisdom of individual members to surface in order to improve the functioning of the whole.

—Charles A. Garfield et al., *Wisdom Circles*

Chapter 1

One Circle Basics

About two years ago Nancy, a senior partner at a national law firm, was invited to join a small group of professional women – primarily for purposes of networking. Although Nancy recalls being hesitant, she now believes the group has changed her life. According to Nancy:

> The group gave me the opportunity to gain perspective and insight into issues that I would not otherwise gain. Often people in leadership roles become isolated, and my group facilitated the discussion of significant issues – in business, family and personal life – in a totally confidential forum. My ability to be more effective as a mother, a wife and lawyer has been enhanced by this group.

This book is about how to bring together such a group of people – who will challenge and support you. This group is called One Circle. This chapter describes what Circles are, the benefits of these Circles and what a Circle is not. It discusses the origins of circles and why the One Circle model works so

19

well. At the end of this chapter are some frequently asked questions about Circles.

What is a Circle?

A Circle is a personal advisory board. It is a group of like-minded people helping each other be their best. This group consists of five to twelve people meeting on a regular basis to discuss their business, their work and their lives. Their primary purpose is to help each other achieve their goals. Such a group usually meets once a month, and the meetings generally last about two hours.

These Circles are primarily for purposes of learning and growing. They are designed to enable each member to solve day-to-day problems and also live a meaningful and balanced life. Circles can be used by almost anyone, including any of the following:

- entrepreneurs wanting to grow their businesses
- executives wanting to become better leaders
- managers wanting to mentor others
- professionals wanting to grow personally and professionally
- parents wanting to be better caregivers and spouses
- people wanting to change careers

Circle meetings follow a particular process that allows for every person to participate, contribute and have their challenges discussed. The process is structured and yet flexible enough to accommodate the ever-changing needs of the individuals in each group.

The benefits of Circles

The strength of Circles lies in the trusting relationships that are developed over time. These relationships create a safe place to have candid conversations and provide the necessary support to enable each member to grow. Circles create a connected community and inviting space where members feel open to sharing stories, experiences and advice. This community in turn provides a broad network of advice, resources and support. Here are some of the specific benefits of Circles.

Circles create solutions and solve problems

Every day we are confronted with new problems. We struggle on our own to find solutions. This can take a significant amount of time and cause enormous frustration.

Some people turn to a small network of colleagues or friends to help them solve personal dilemmas. Although these networks are very helpful, they have several weaknesses. They are not always available, they are not always neutral, and they often come with strings attached. These collegial relations are based on a vague system of give-and-take and can generally only be used in certain contexts and situations. For example, an accountant might not want to phone his mother when having trouble with new software.

A Circle consists of people whose *responsibility* is to help you. Each person in the Circle is there to help you succeed. If one cannot help, another likely can. Circle members do this both in the meeting and after the meeting. A Circle is a place for open and candid conversations about all sorts of challenges or problems. It is a place for diagnosing problems; it is a place for unfettered imagination and creative ideas; it is

21

a place for canvassing different options and ultimately selecting the one that works best.

A Circle provides a place for the sharing of unique and rich worldly experiences, stories, opinions and feelings. It brings together the cumulative thoughts, opinions and ideas of each of its members. The quality and quantity of advice and suggestions is limited only by the combined life experiences of the group.

Circles provide wise advice, information and suggestions

As we grow personally and professionally in business and careers, we increasingly value wise advice, practical and relevant information, and creative suggestions. To stay alive and vital in business and life, we need a continual flow of this information.

For this advice to be valuable, the provider must, at a minimum, understand who you are and what you want. Indeed, the best advice is usually gained from someone who has known you for a long time and understands your uniqueness, your goals and your personal circumstances.

However, we are all so busy that we often do not have the time to keep others up to speed on what we are doing. Our lives and businesses are constantly changing, and it is very difficult to keep others in the loop. A few lunches here or there with a few close colleagues are not enough. Those who could provide us with great advice are extraordinarily rare.

One Circle is a group of people who, over time, learn about you, about your business, and about your personal goals and aspirations. Because they meet with you on a regular basis, you do not need to keep reminding them about who you are and what you do. Eventually each person becomes a valuable source of advice, information and suggestions, both inside and outside the Circle.

Circles generate contacts and resources

Whether we work in organizational settings or on our own, we all need others to help build our businesses and our careers. Businesses need to know about their competitors, suppliers and markets. They need a continual flow of new ideas and customers, both to stay in business and to excel. At an individual level we need information about alternative careers and contacts, and at a personal level we need information about everything from the names of plumbers to those of medical specialists.

Many people belong to clubs, associations and networking groups to meet their need to generate contacts. They talk to others and hope to glean some nugget at each event or meeting. These events, however, rarely meet all their needs. This is because most groups meet infrequently, consist of an ever-changing mix of people, and have vague objectives. The typical lunch or after-work networking meeting rarely provides sufficient time to speak to others, yet alone understand what others do or how you can help each other.

As a result it can take years to develop dependable relationships. By contrast, in a constant Circle, whether a group as small as five or as large as ten, there are usually enough leads or ideas about leads generated to keep everyone satisfied. The principle is a lot like the theory of six degrees of separation first proposed in 1929 and popularized by a 1990 movie.

Circles develop skills and transfer wisdom

As humans we are lifelong learners. We are curious by nature, and without learning we stagnate. We learn about things from books and teachers. We learn skills and how to apply what we know by watching others and practicing. We also learn from hearing about how others do things. We learn tacit or practical knowledge by word of mouth.

A Circle helps members develop knowledge, skills, and new ways of thinking about things and doing things. Skills gained in a Circle range from basic problem-solving skills to communication skills and practical work-related skills. More advanced skills include leadership skills, marketing skills, speaking skills and even coping skills. A Circle also provides a place to experiment or test things out before putting them into action. Through ongoing conversations, best practices (and worst practices) are passed along.

Circles help achieve goals and balance

We all have hopes and dreams. Each person comes to the Circle with some goals and perhaps a vision of their ideal life. We all set tasks and go about trying to accomplish them day to day. However, year after year, many of these goals remain unaccomplished, and we wonder why. Many of us struggle both with setting clear goals and sticking to them. Although we could be more effective and efficient, we end up in a bit of a rut and somehow get off track.

One goal that many people share is the goal of living a balanced life. As baby boomers advance in their careers and businesses, they begin to question the long hours and the emphasis on work. These sentiments are shared by the emerging Generation X, who are looking not only for balance but also for meaningful work.

In a Circle every person is dedicated to helping each other achieve success and balance – whatever that might mean to each person on an individual basis. The Circle helps its members clarify their goals and set priorities. The Circle then holds each person accountable for those goals and provides necessary support. Even the most self-driven individual welcomes the support of a Circle.

Circles offer support and connection

Our society has become increasingly individualistic. As described in the book *Wisdom Circles,* this emphasis on the individual has become a liability in North America:

> During the last four hundred years of human history, tremendous emphasis has been laid on the development of the individual. Wise teachers have encouraged us to know ourselves, trust our inner authority, try the road not taken and fulfill our potential. Western psychology has given us a body of literature on why we need to "individuate," that is search for the essence of our own uniqueness. Unfortunately, any asset pushed too far becomes a liability.[1]

To compound matters, as corporate structures give way to more project-based work, the world of contract workers and entrepreneurs is on the rise. Today more than ever people are becoming consultants and business owners. These individuals miss the camaraderie offered inside corporations and often feel isolated. Many are looking for a sense of connection

25

or belonging. They are searching for ways to come together for support and connection.

Research suggests that this sense of connection is critical to well-being, and much of our stress can be attributed to a lack of a sense of community. People need to feel they are part of a community to which they belong and contribute. In his book *American Mania*, Peter Whybrow describes how Americans are starving for connection. He suggests that many Americans have pursued happiness by accumulating material wealth and have forgotten the real source of happiness: intimacy. He says:

> It is intimacy, not materialism that buffers the stress of everyday living. Meaning is found in the social bond. Attachment to others serves survival in infancy, and empathetic understanding facilitates adaptation throughout life. Feelings of happiness are tied to intimacy and are dependent on the reinforcing presence of companions and friendship.[2]

Whybrow explains how Adam Smith's economic philosophy was based on a balance between commercial liberty and the social structures that are rapidly eroding in North America. Apparently Smith felt that human envy and a tendency toward compulsive craving, if left unchecked, would destroy empathetic feeling and the neighborly concerns essential to his economic model and a free market's successful operation.

Robert Lane, a professor of political science at Yale, in his book *The Loss of Happiness in Market Democracies*, described the decline of American community to a state of psychic malnutrition – a kind of famine of warm interpersonal relations, of easy-to-reach neighbors, of encircling, inclusive member-ships amid a life of material abundance. The book *Bowling Alone,* by Robert D. Putnam, also describes the decline of social groups across the United States over the past century.

Although there are many ways in which people come together, such as networking meetings, book clubs and dinner groups, these meet only some of the needs of busy profession-al people. Causal networking does not allow for deeper dis-cussions, book clubs rarely discuss work life, and dinner groups are mostly just for fun and meeting new people. At the same time, the corporate world can often feel uninviting and frightening. It is rare today to find a healthy and supportive work environment, and the statistics show this is taking a toll.

People need to feel safe to be creative and to reach their full potential. Circles create places where this can happen. In a Circle members are challenged yet supported. Members chal-lenge each other's thinking, beliefs and actions in a supportive manner. They reconcile what you say with what you do, and they hold you accountable in way that encourages your devel-opment.

What Circles are not

Circles are different from social groups, sports groups and educational groups, and it helps to know how they are distinct.

A Circle is not a social group

Many people belong to social clubs or more loosely defined groups such as extended families or community groups. Many belong to book clubs and dinner clubs. Although these groups might discuss issues and problems, they are different from

Circles in two main ways. First, they are constructed mostly for pleasure. Their main outcome is a sense of fun or happiness. Therefore, as we all know, when the conversation gets a bit controversial, a social convener will quickly de-escalate the conversation to ensure no one gets insulted or hurt. Many potentially authentic conversations thus get pushed aside to maintain a level of comfort or social decorum. In Circles, this does not happen.

The other reason social groups differ from Circles relates to accountability. In most social groups you may enter and leave the group freely. Although your absence may be noted, you are not generally compelled to attend or to account for your actions. In a Circle, your absence is always noticed, and you are committed to that Circle.

A Circle is not a therapy group

There will be times when an individual in a Circle will confront a serious life crisis such as divorce or death. The Circle is an appropriate place to share these circumstances, learn from them and gain some support. The Circle is not, however, designed to provide therapy. In these situations there must be a balance between providing emotional support and meeting the needs of the other members.

The Circle process ensures that conversations stay focused in two specific ways. Since each person is responsible for maintaining the conversation, if an individual feels that a conversation is getting off track, that person must speak up. Each Circle creates their own unique Circle Purpose Statement that describes the particular focus of the group. If a conversation seems to be going on a tangent, the members can remind the group of their purpose and talk about how to keep focused.

A Circle is not group coaching

Many executive and life coaches use group coaching to help their clients. These groups are different from Circles in several ways. First, a coach selects the group on the basis of who needs coaching as opposed to how the members can help one another. Second, a coach usually steps into a leadership role and often provides coaching throughout the meeting. Third, coached groups tend to be fairly short-term and are not designed to be self-sustaining. They are often set up by a coach and tend to last only as long as the members feel they need the help of a coach.

These differences indicate the ways in which Circles can be so meaningful and long-lasting. Indeed, Circles have historic foundations.

The origins of Circles

Circles date back to monolithic times. According to many experts, circles are not a current fad but rather a combination of both ancient and modern wisdom – about how to keep human relationships alive, free, open and constructive, as described here by Beverly Engel:

> In time the circle became the primary social, political, spiritual structure as evidenced in paintings, carvings, petroglyphs, runes, crafts and, later, architecture. We see the remnants of circle-based cultures among indigenous peoples all around the world. For example, the Inuit of the Arctic still meet in circle as do most Native American tribes.[3]

Most of the Circles in existence today would be considered spiritual-type circles or aboriginal-type Circles. In her book *Women Circling the Earth,* Beverly Engel describes many of the emerging types of Circles, including council circles, crones' circles, creative circles, dream circles, empowerment circles, peacemaking circles, PeerSpirit circles, sacred circles, simplicity circles and wisdom circles. Each of these is directed at a particular audience for a particular purpose.

Other groups closely related to Circles are mastermind groups, dream teams and peer-mentoring groups. In 1932 Napoleon Hill coined the term "mastermind groups." Hill conducted research on some of the wealthiest men in history and came to discover that almost all of them were members of various "mastermind" groups. He described these groups as being powerful think tanks specifically formed to provide the expertise that businesspeople needed to excel. Since that time, mastermind groups and peer-based think tanks have emerged in many different fields. One version is the so-called barn-raising, where a group of entrepreneurs, business owners and executives will get together to provide feedback to an individual on a new business idea or concept.

Another type of group related to Circles are dream teams, a term coined by Barbara Sher, an author and career expert. In her best-selling book *Wishcraft,* Sher suggests that people in transition or between jobs can seriously benefit from a group. The aim of dream teams is to help people in transition think creatively about who they are and their ideal job. A more recent version of dream teams is offered by author Cheryl Richardson's *Take Time for Your Life* groups.

Yet another modern form of groups is peer mentoring, which grew out of the counseling field. For many years psychologists and counselors have used peer groups to help people solve psychological problems. The bulk of the peer-mentoring programs were established in high schools in North America, and today many high school counselors use peer mentoring regularly.

There are many types of peer-mentoring groups today, ranging from Alcoholics Anonymous to exclusive executive programs, such as the forum used by the Young Presidents' Organization. Although similar to mastermind groups, peer-mentoring groups are not generally constructed with a particular mix of experts. Their focus tends to be on mentoring individual members through difficult times, and they are usually facilitated by a leader or guide. They often have a set start and ending period.

Circles are different from these groups in three main ways. First, Circles are not limited to any particular purpose and can be used for almost any purpose by any group. The group itself decides on its unique purpose. It has no set time frame, and it can last as long as the group wishes.

Second, Circles are self-sustaining. Although Circles can be facilitated by an outsider, in a typical Circle the leadership role is rotated. This reinforces the Circle Principles of shared leadership and shared ownership. This self-sustaining quality has many benefits. It makes Circles easy to set up, inexpensive to operate, and flexible enough to adjust to the shifting needs of the group.

Third, and most importantly, Circles provide the sense of safety necessary to build trust, create significant conversations and develop deeper relationships. This safe place also provides a type of incubator that allows individuals to become more empowered.

The following chart compares some of the better-known types of groups to the One Circle model.

Circles compared to other groups

	One Circle	Mastermind and peer-mentoring groups	Networking and social groups	Corporate teams
Membership	Any person who wants help solving problems and achieving their goals	A select mix of business professionals, often based on corporate position or income	Friends and business acquaintances	Those assigned to the group by management
Size	Consistent group of 5 to 12 people	Consistent group of 10 to 15 people	More than 20 and often over 100	Depends on the group or the project
Purpose	A shared purpose as decided by the group	To share business advice and expertise	To meet other people	To deliver a service or product or accomplish a task
Duration	As long as the group wishes. Groups meet once a month and are usually self-facilitated	Usually monthly meetings over one year, subject to renewal	Usually monthly meetings with annual membership	Ongoing or until a project is complete
Glue	The Circle Principles, Practices and Process	Formal commitment and membership fee	New people in varied businesses	Required by job
Cost	No fee.	Variety of fees, depending on service offered	Variety of membership fees	No fee

Why Circles work

There are three main reasons why Circles work. As humans we enjoy being with others, we are more creative in groups, and we are more courageous when with others.

People enjoy the human connection of groups

The main reason Circles work so well is because people generally like being with other people. We are by nature social. We also need to interact with each other and tend to be happier and work better when with others. Indeed, research shows that human interaction is necessary for normal human development and that loneliness, a sense of isolation and even serious illnesses can be caused by lack of human interaction.

On the more positive side, people generally want to help others. Most people, when asked for help, feel drawn to assist. When someone asks for our help, it is often difficult for us to refuse, but more importantly, our helping almost always provides us with a sense of satisfaction.

People tend to be more creative in groups

Research has repeatedly shown the power of group thinking. Groups tend to create not just more, but better ideas than any one group member.

As human beings, our minds work in predictable ways. We form patterns of thinking and, when confronted with new situations, tend to apply our tried-and-true methods of solving these problems. A disadvantage of this, of course, is that when we get stuck, we cannot seem to get unstuck. By working in a group, individuals are able to break free of patterns, adopt new ways of looking at things and become more open.

33

Synergies emerge as people open up and combine their thoughts and energy.

An example of group synergy can be demonstrated through a brainstorming exercise. Each of the group members is asked to simply state ideas that come to mind. Each idea stimulates another, and so on. By the end of the exercise most of the members are surprised not only by the ideas that have emerged, but by the realization that their personal assumptions would have prevented many of the ideas from surfacing at all.

Group synergy is enhanced in situations where people feel safe. In these situations, individuals tend to be more willing to say what is on their mind. In a safe place creativity tends to emerge more easily.

People tend to be more courageous in groups

The world is not always an inviting place. Each of us welcomes a harbor from an often stormy world of work and sometimes difficult relations. When we are alone we are limited to our own resources and thus have a tendency not to take many risks. We are not as courageous as we might like. People in groups tend to be more courageous and take on more risks. This is due to two factors.

First, people generally feel safer when surrounded by others. When in a group, individuals tend to share or spread the responsibility among the individuals. For example, feelings of both disappointment and success are spread out over the group, decreasing their impact on any one person.

Second, a group provides direct support. Each person, as a group member, contributes in some way to each other's decisions and actions. Thus each person tends to feel committed to that decision or action. If one member fails, there is a shared sense of loss. If one member succeeds, there is a shared sense of accomplishment. As a result of these feelings in a group, individuals tend to be more daring and creative.

Another interesting phenomenon is that people tend to have more courage for others than for themselves. Others do not feel your hesitation and fears in the same way you do. They can often see things more objectively and make challenges more manageable.

Circles at a glance

By way of both summing up this chapter and filling in a few details, here are some frequently asked questions and answers about Circles.

What is a Circle?

A Circle is a group of five to twelve people who get together for the purpose of helping each other solve problems and achieve their goals. It is a personal advisory board for work and life. The group meets on a regular basis to discuss their business, work and life. These meetings generally last one to three hours.

What is the purpose of a Circle?

Circles are intended primarily to tap the synergy of a group to help each person in the Circle creatively solve problems. The Circle is designed to enable all members to be their best and live successful and balanced lives. Circles can be used by almost anyone and specifically benefit the following individuals:

- entrepreneurs wanting to grow their businesses
- executives wanting to become better leaders
- managers wanting to mentor others
- professionals wanting to grow personally and professionally
- parents wanting to be better caregivers and spouses
- people wanting to change careers

What are the benefits of a Circle?

The strength of Circles lies in the trusting relationships that are developed over time. These relationships create a safe place to have candid conversations and provide the necessary support to enable each member to grow. The specific benefits a Circle provides are as follows:

- create solutions and solve problems
- share wise advice and information
- generate contacts and resources
- develop skills and continuously learn
- help achieve goals and balance
- provide support and connection

How does a Circle work?

The group agrees to the fundamental Circle Principles (see chapter 2) and follows the Circle Process (see chapter 5), which allows every person to participate and contribute. The process is both structured and flexible enough to accommodate the ever-changing needs of the individuals in that group.

How long will a Circle last?

Circles are designed to last for months and even years.

Who will be in my Circle?

Each group decides who will be in their Circle after considering certain criteria, such as motivation to join and the purpose of the Circle. Ideally members should have similar goals and noncompeting interests. Once a Circle is formed, new members may join only if every person in the group agrees.

How often do Circles meet?

Circles meet on a regular basis, usually once or twice a month over several years.

What will I have to do in a Circle?

You will need to show up for all meetings set by the group, and you will need to commit to the five fundamental Circle Principles: equality, confidentiality, commitment, shared ownership and shared leadership. These principles are discussed in more detail in chapter 2.

Who runs a Circle?

A Circle is always facilitated by a Circle Guide. This guide can either be a member of the Circle or an external facilitator. If the guide is a member, this role should be rotated so that each member participates in leading the Circle at some point. If the guide is external, they should have some experience with Circles.

What should I expect at the first meeting?

The focus of every Circle is on building strong relationships. Therefore the process is deliberately paced to allow for bonds to grow naturally. The first few meetings are dedicated to getting to know each other, clarifying expectations and learning about the Circle Process. Agendas for the first six meetings can be found in chapters 6 and 7.

How are Circles different from other groups?

Unlike many other groups, Circles are resilient, encourage significant conversations and build trusting relationships. The unique Circle Principles, Practices and Process provide the sense of safety necessary to enable members to learn and grow.

Circles are different from many groups in three main ways. First, Circles are not limited to any particular purpose and can be used for almost any purpose by any group. The group itself decides its unique purpose. It has no set time frame and it can last as long as the group wishes.

Second, Circles are self-sustaining. Although Circles can be facilitated by an outsider, in a typical Circle the leadership role is rotated. This reinforces the Circle Principles of shared leadership and shared ownership. This self-sustaining quality has many benefits. It makes Circles easy to set up, inexpensive to operate, and flexible enough to adjust to the shifting needs of the group.

Third, and most importantly, Circles provide the sense of safety necessary to build trust, create significant conversations and develop deeper relationships. This safe place also provides a type of incubator that allows individuals to become more empowered.

Chapter 2

One Circle Principles

*The energy of a circle can create a space that
can allow for the unorthodox to enter and the
unexpected to happen.*

—Sedonia Cahill and Joshua Halpern,
The Ceremonial Circle

*Don't judge his actions by what you would do.
You are not living completely within truth
as he is.* —Rumi

The One Circle model is based on five fundamental principles. Each member agrees to these principles before joining the Circle, and the entire Circle Process is based on them. As you come to apply the principles you will begin to understand why Circles are so unique. By adhering to these principles you increase your chances of having richer conversations, deeper relationships and a longer lasting Circle.

This chapter describes the five Circle Principles – equality, confidentiality, commitment, shared ownership and shared leadership – and the role of the Circle Guide. At the end of the chapter is a summary of the One Circle Principles that you may wish to circulate to members before they join the Circle.

Equality

The foundation of any Circle is equality. This means that although we are all unique, no one person in the group is more important or valuable than another person. Each person must be respected simply for being a person and a part of the Circle. In *The Millionth Circle,* Jean Bolen writes:

> A Circle is non-hierarchical – that is what equality is like. This is how a culture behaves when it listens and learns from everyone in it.[1]

Starhawk, in her book *Dreaming the Dark,* describes the equality of circles in the following way:

> In a circle each person's face can be seen, each person's voice can be heard and valued. All points on a circle are equidistant from its center: that is its definition, and its function – to distribute energy equally.[2]

In the Circle occupational titles and the status that may be attached to your position have no weight. Each member is valued not on the basis of their accomplishments or their possessions, but as an important individual and a critical contributor to the Circle. As stated by Cecile Andrews in her book *The Circle of Simplicity:*

People will participate fully only when they respond as equals. When you are in a subordinate position, you distrust your own judgment and learn to sabotage those with more power. When you are in a superior position, you become arrogant and close yourself off to new information. You quit listening and learning and become defensive and hostile if anyone questions you.[3]

Related to the idea of equality is the idea of equal contribution or participation. Although no one is forced to participate in a Circle, the Circle must provide an equal opportunity to participate. This participation, even if in silence, is important to what happens in the Circle.

Equality also means accepting that we are all related in some way and are thus interconnected to each other and to the world in which we live. According to ancient circle teachings, the shape of the circle affirms this interconnectedness.

As a member of the Circle each person commits to respect each other person. In a practical sense this includes acknowledging and appreciating each member's feelings, beliefs and actions. At times a person may not like what another member says, but each must show respect.

Being an equal in a group can be difficult for some people. One of the reasons relates to power. Some people are accustomed to having complete control and directing others. They are assertive and feel most comfortable when they are giving instructions or advice. Others prefer to sit back and allow others to lead. They prefer to let others direct the conversation and make decisions. Regardless of your accustomed relationship to power, the important thing to keep in mind is that power is always at play in every group. Although not a bad thing, if it prevents members from speaking up, it must be recognized and addressed. Otherwise, the Circle will begin to behave like a car with one flat wheel. The full and equal participation of all members keeps the Circle in balance and effective.

Confidentiality

In order to create a safe, trusting and nonthreatening environment, confidentiality in a Circle is critical. This means keeping anything that is said at the Circle meeting confidential to yourself, unless specific permission is given to disclose it.

It also means keeping the names of the members of that group confidential. Although outsiders, such as family members, may know about your involvement in a Circle, it is best to keep the names of the members in your Circle confidential. The risk of telling those close to us about the members is that friends and family may forget that they are not to tell others. Before you know it, someone from across town knows you are in a Circle. If someone really wants to know who is in your group, it is best to ask the group whether they want their names disclosed.

In situations where others may urge you to disclose information about your Circle, ask yourself the following questions:

- Why does the other person need this information?
- What are their motives?
- How might the information be used?
- Why do I feel compelled to share the information?

- What are my motives?
- How can I talk about the Circle without sharing others' stories?
- How can I limit this discussion to my personal stories?
- Could I tell the others in the Circle about what I shared?

To reinforce the principle of confidentiality, members may wish to formally adopt this Circle Principle in writing. Members may formally adopt any or all of the other principles as well.

Commitment

As a member of a Circle you must commit to being a member of the group. In practical terms this means showing up and participating. By joining the Circle each person is committing to the other members and to the Circle Process.

Each person commits to being open, honest and supportive. This includes contributing in a constructive way and being candid but kind. It includes being able to listen to feedback from others.

The commitment to the process is a respect for the Circle Principles, Practices and Process. This means understanding the process, following the agreed-upon rules, and being responsible and accountable for any breaches.

Some Circles also agree to certain ground rules for meetings. These rules can provide comfort to some and can be brought up as a gentle reminder if the rules are breached. Here are some examples of these rules.

- Be on time and present at each meeting.

- Be responsible for your own comfort.

- If you are going to be late, call someone.

- Be responsible for expressing your own needs.

- Be honest and open.

- Own your experiences by saying "I," not "we."

- Stay within time limits.

- Express appreciation to the Circle Guide.

Shared ownership

The fourth Circle Principle, shared ownership, means that every member in the Circle shares in the design and functioning of the Circle. Each person shares responsibility for creating a Circle that meets their needs and maintaining the Circle over its life.

Each member must help to decide on a mutually acceptable purpose and must select a process that works best in their circumstances.

Each member is personally responsible for holding the Circle together. This means contributing to the group and remaining aware of the growth or deterioration of the group. Each member must speak up when things seem to be moving in the wrong direction. If the Circle is a success, each member can be congratulated. If the Circle is a failure, each person must take equal responsibility. No one person owns or leads the Circle. All contribute and help guide the process in ways that will strengthen the Circle. In her book *Dreaming the Dark,*

Starhawk describes the typical corporate meeting and what happens when the principle of shared ownership is absent:

> In most hierarchical groups, at any given time in a meeting, a very few people will be doing all the talking. The others will be silent – sometimes impressed, more often bored, doodling, writing letters to absent friends, or thinking about what to eat for dinner. The few talkers end up making the decisions and formulating the plans; the others abdicate or feel subtly discounted. When groups work in this fashion, they reinforce the thought-forms of estrangement. Members get the idea that some people are valuable and others are not.[4]

One way shared ownership plays out in Circles is that all decisions are made through consensus. Members decide matters together without a vote or majority rule. If they cannot decide, they gather more information and put off the decision until the time is right.

Shared leadership

In a Circle every member is a leader. There are no hierarchies, and the leadership role is shared. Each member has the opportunity and responsibility to take the Circle in a certain direction. Eventually each person will find their own unique way of leading as a member.

To ensure shared leadership, it is recommended that each member be responsible for taking on the role of the Circle Guide at some time. This role is described later (see chapter 5) but essentially includes arranging meetings and guiding the Circle process at the Circle meeting. Even those who have had minimal experience in a leadership or facilitation role can guide the Circle process fairly easily.

The principle of shared leadership goes with the principles of equality and shared ownership. In North America we have grown up in a culture where we value independence and one-person leadership. As a result we tend to define leaders as people with authoritarian characteristics and often rely on these leaders to provide direction. These characteristics are being challenged by modern managers, and more inclusive leadership styles are now well recognized. For Circles, the style does not matter so much as the opportunity for each person to play a leadership role and in doing so apply their own unique style. Members must realize that by depending on one person to lead, others can become disempowered and have their own leadership abilities grow rusty.

The ideal situation is to rotate the role of Circle Guide – usually for a few months at a time. This allows each member of the group to play the role over time. It allows each member to learn the necessary skills of leading the Circle and demystifies the role of the guide. It also spreads out the responsibilities and time commitment. Most importantly, however, it ensures that each member is treated equally and shares in the power. The main drawback is that some members may prefer not to facilitate and may not be skilled at it. In this case, they may wish to wait until they have had an opportunity to watch others in the role before taking it on.

An external Circle Guide is also an option and can be very useful for the first few meetings. An experienced Circle Guide can act as the host while the group is forming or until the members develop the relationships that will ultimately hold the Circle together.

An external guide is typically responsible for arranging the meetings, setting them up and ensuring the process is adhered to. Here are some of the advantages of using an external Circle Guide.

* Members save time in scheduling and setting up meetings.

* A skilled guide can educate the members quickly on the Circle Process.

* Members can focus on the conversation as opposed to the process.

* An experienced guide can answer questions so good habits can form early.

* Members can watch and learn from seeing the guide in action.

* An external guide can build the foundation for future meetings.

The ideal guide is someone who is completely neutral but familiar with the Circle Principles, Practices and Process. This person will essentially be a process person and will not contribute to the substance of your conversation. This is important because the Circle process functions best without any active facilitation by the Circle Guide. The guide must be careful not to disempower members or to detract from the fundamental principles – especially shared ownership and shared leadership. At the minimum the guide should be skilled at each of the Circle Practices and particularly listening, speaking and guiding.

Although some more established Circles prefer to have no guide, this tends to be problematic. Even those groups that feel confident that they can collectively lead the process will at some point struggle. Difficulties Circles encounter that require the help of a guide include dealing with power imbalances, outspoken members and strong emotions as well as bringing in new members. Handling these difficulties is discussed further in chapter 8. At a point of difficulty it is awkward to invite back an external guide, since the move suggests something is wrong.

Another option is co-guiding. This involves two members sharing the role of Circle Guide. This can work well but can also be cumbersome. One way to make it work is by splitting the responsibilities. For example, one person could be responsible for the Opening and one for the Closing of the meeting. To share the role of guide requires significant cooperation and communication between the two. It would be inappropriate to have any conversations about the role during the Circle and, of course, any power struggles would be problematic.

Summary of One Circle Principles

This summary of the Circle Principles can be provided to members at the first Circle meeting and can be used as a basis for discussion. Some Circles prefer to write their own version of these principles and have each member sign the document to demonstrate their commitment to them.

Equality

Circle members believe that each person in a Circle is equal. They agree that no one person in the group is more important or valuable than another, and they agree to do the following:

- respect each person simply for being a person and a part of the Circle

- value each person as a critical contributor to the Circle

- allow each person an equal opportunity to participate

- reinforce the connection between members

Confidentiality

Circle members understand that confidentiality is critical to the functioning of the Circle and agree to do as follows:

- keep everything said in the Circle confidential

- ask members whether they wish to disclose any information

- keep the names of members confidential

Commitment

Circle members must commit to the Circle, the Circle Process and to one another. They understand the importance of confidentiality and agree to undertake the following:

- commit to being a member of the Circle

- show up to meetings and participate

- learn the Circle Principles, Practices and Process

- be open, honest and supportive

- follow any agreed-upon rules

- be responsible and accountable

Shared ownership

Circle members agree to share in the ownership of the Circle. They agree to do as follows:

- participate in the design and creation of the Circle
- be responsible for the functioning and maintenance of the Circle
- be aware of the growth or deterioration of the group
- speak up when things seem to be moving in the wrong direction
- make decisions by consensus

Shared leadership

Circle members agree to share in the leadership of the Circle and agree to the following tenets:

- Every member is a leader.
- There are no hierarchies.
- The leadership role is shared.
- Members share the role of Circle Guide.

These foundational principles keep Circles together and on track and when used in conjunction with the Circle Practices and Circle Process, create a safe place where meaningful conversations can happen. The next chapter describes how to get a Circle started.

....

Chapter 3

Getting Started

Many hundreds of circles are composed of people who gather together in each other's homes to facilitate self-discovery and build compassionate community, and these circles give them support in handling the rest their lives.

—Charles A. Garfield et al., *Wisdom Circles*

Before creating a Circle you need to consider several things, such as why you want a Circle and what your Circle might look like. You must then sort out the logistics. This chapter describes the things you need to consider in getting started and specifically answers the following questions:

- Why do you want a Circle?
- Where will you meet?
- How long will you meet?
- When will you meet?

- Who will you invite?
- Who will be the temporary Circle Guide?

Toward the end of the chapter is a script you can use when inviting members and a checklist for use when planning your Circle.

Why do you want a Circle?

Many people belong to groups such as business associations, networking groups, book clubs and community clubs. Each of these groups provides something to its members. For example, a book club might provide an intellectually stimulating environment or an opportunity to get together with other book lovers. A networking group might provide a stream of leads to develop your business or an opportunity to meet other professionals.

Although every person will have a different reason for joining a Circle, there are three main reasons for joining: to solve day-to-day problems, to achieve goals, and to continuously learn and grow. Every Circle is designed to meet these three general purposes.

Each Circle, however, has more specific purposes and typically gets started with a specific goal or purpose in mind. This purpose is usually driven by the particular problems each of the members is confronting at that time. For example, a group of small-business owners might form a Circle to deal with growing their businesses. A group of managers in an organization might form a Circle to discuss the challenges of managing employees and projects.

The following is a list of some typical Circles and their main goals.

Entrepreneur Circles

Main goal: Business development and growth.

- I want to expand my business.
- I want to learn how to deal with personnel issues.
- I want a stronger business network.
- I want more access to leads and resources.
- I want to better market and promote my business.

Executive Circles

Main goal: Effective leadership and decision making.

- I want to excel as a leader or business owner.
- I want to work more effectively and efficiently.
- I want to learn how other executives manage.
- I need help with day-to-day problems.
- I want to leave a legacy.

Corporate mentoring Circles

Main goal: Professional development and succession.

- I want to learn new skills.
- I want to know what it takes to succeed.
- I want someone to mentor me.
- I want support in reaching my aspirations.
- I want to be a better leader.

Professional Circles

Main goal: Success and balance.

- I want to excel in my career or business.
- I want to find balance between home and work.
- I want to learn how to be more assertive.
- I want to learn how other women manage.
- I want to feel connected to others.

Parenting Circles

Main goal: Success as a parent.

- I want to learn from the experiences of others.
- I want to solve my parenting problems.
- I want to be a great parent and partner.
- I want constructive relationships.
- I want to feel connected to a community.

Career change Circles

Main goal: A successful career shift.

- I want to network better.
- I want to learn job-finding skills.
- I want support and ideas from others.
- I want to find meaningful work.
- I want to overcome obstacles.

As you can see, the goals of any Circle are both wide-ranging and unique. Your Circle purpose will likely be a combination of these aforementioned goals. You will define the purpose of your own Circle in your first few meetings.

In addition to identifying some goals before you get started, it is useful to consider how a Circle could most benefit you. This involves identifying some of the practical reasons why you want to join a Circle – in both the short and the long term. You can do this by describing how a Circle could help you today and how it might help you in, say, five years. Complete the following statements to help you identify your own reasons for joining a Circle:

- I'd really like someone to help me come up with ideas for...

- I could definitely use some help with...

- I'd love to brainstorm some thoughts about...

- I really need some practical advice about...

- I could really use some support right now. Then I could...

- If only I knew someone who knew more about...

Once you have a fairly clear idea about what you want and need, you can draft a personal purpose statement. This will form the foundation of your group discussions about your Circle Purpose Statement. Here are some examples of quite different personal purpose statements.

- *I am a senior executive.* I have been working in the same organization for over fifteen years. I need a constant source of new ideas and want to be better able to manage my time and priorities. I also need help in dealing with conflict. I would love to know how other executives deal with their problems. I would like to know the secret to keeping good people around me.

- *I am a small-business owner.* I have been in business for five years and feel that the business is stalling. I am having trouble keeping good support staff and can't seem to find partners to help me grow. In the short term I would like my Circle to help me refocus and grow my business. In the long term I would like my Circle to help me sell the business and retire.

- *I am a lawyer and parent.* I am working full time and love my career but feel that I am in constant motion. I feel like I never get ahead and I rarely have time for myself. I would like my Circle to help me become more effective and efficient. I would like help in building my law practice. I want to slow down yet keep my income growing. I also have aging parents and am concerned about their care.

- *I am a manager in a big corporation.* I have been here for four years and want to move up in the corporation. I seem to be stalled or blocked and want to know how to get ahead faster. I would love to meet with other managers and executives on a regular basis and learn about what they did and continue to do. I could also benefit from some wise advice about how to deal with some issues I am facing as a manager.

Once you have decided why you want a Circle and know how it could help you, you need to figure out the logistics of holding a Circle meeting.

Where will you meet?

The location you select can be important for many reasons and specifically in relation to comfort, confidentiality and access. Since the main aim of the Circle is to have candid conversations, the ideal location is one where everyone feels comfortable and where conversations cannot be overheard or interrupted. Also, if the location is easy to get to, the odds of members showing up will increase.

For the first few gatherings it is best to hold the Circle meetings in the same location, since people tend to feel safer in a place to which they have become accustomed. After that it is best to alternate locations periodically to allow others to host the meetings and for a change of scenery. Locations could include a member's home, a boardroom, a quiet restaurant or a meeting room at a community center.

How long will you meet?

There are three parts to this question: How long do you want your meetings to last? How often do you wish to meet? and How long do you want your group to last as One Circle? Here is a sample answer:

Duration: 2 hours

Frequency of meetings: Once a month

Duration of the Circle: At least one year

Most Circles meet for two to three hours. For a group of up to eight people, this allows enough time for full participation and a rich conversation. If the group is larger, more time is necessary. It is important to allow enough time. Relationships and comfort levels need to develop naturally.

One interesting thing about Circles is that meetings tend to last longer at the beginning, mostly so people can get to know each other. The first few meetings are almost completely dedicated to finding out more about each other and learning how to conduct a Circle. Over time, although the meetings are more efficient, the members tend to want to spend more time together, so will either extend their meeting times or increase the number of meetings!

Most Circles meet once a month, primarily for convenience. This schedule allows the members time between meetings to apply what they have learned and report back. If the members have a lot to discuss or wish to get their Circle started faster, they may wish to schedule more meetings.

It is best to not wait longer than six weeks between meetings. This can cause a breakdown in communication and relationships. If meetings are not held often enough, there is a loss of continuity. People tend to lose the connection and interest or simply forget why they are meeting at all. Six weeks can be a long time between meetings.

When will you meet?

Besides location and frequency, another thing to consider is the scheduling of meetings. Often the availability of the members determines when they will meet and for how long. The most common meeting times are these:

- early in the morning
- over lunchtime
- immediately after work
- in the evening

The first meeting is always the hardest to schedule, but once the members decide on a day and a time, they are able to schedule the rest of the meetings well in advance. An effective Circle requires that every member be in attendance. One member missing can shift the conversation and the chemistry significantly.

Most Circles come up with a way to deal with a member who cannot make a meeting. For example, if a Circle must be cancelled, that member will be responsible for rescheduling the meeting within the next two weeks.

Whom will you invite?

The size and composition of your Circle is fairly important to its success. Ultimately you want a group that will gel and stay together for a long time. These people will help you achieve your goals and support you as you encounter difficulties in your business and life. Although a Circle can consist of almost any combination of people, the right combination can definitely make a Circle more successful.

The selection process is much like selecting the guests for a party. You might start with the purpose of the party and invite the people appropriate for that purpose. If your purpose is to welcome a new family to the neighborhood, your invitation list would likely include a cross-section of neighbors with varying interests. You would likely invite those who have some things in common, but not so much in common that they might make the conversation dull.

The secret to selecting the ideal group is related specifically to the ultimate purpose of your Circle and your particular needs at this particular time. There are also a few practical factors you need to consider. In regard to group size, Starhawk in her book *Dreaming the Dark* emphasizes the need to keep the group small:

> To empower individuals, groups must be small enough so that within them we can each have time to speak, to be heard, to know each other personally. The time we give to a person and the depth of attention we pay to her/his words and feelings are measures of the worth we accord her/him. We enact the theology of immanence, the belief that we are each inherently valuable, by creating groups in which each person is given time and attention – given respect.[1]

Practical factors you should consider when selecting members of your Circle include getting the right mix, people's motivations, members' stage of life, and any perceived conflict or competition.

Mix it up

In forming a Circle, it is best to include a mix of people. This is simply because you will want your Circle to have access to as many different experiences and perspectives as possible. If you select only people like yourself, your ability to create breakthrough ideas will be more limited. Here are several factors to consider when thinking about selecting members:

- personalities, such as introverted or extroverted
- experiences, such as local or international
- industries, such as service or manufacturing
- occupations, such as private or public sector
- employment, such as entrepreneurs or employees

Motivation

An important factor when inviting members is their motive for joining. Often those attracted to Circles are not completely aware of why they want to join a Circle. Some people simply sense that the time is right. I often hear things like "I just feel it is time for me to do this," or "I feel this is necessary if I truly want to be successful," or "I have tried everything and I am burnt out." Often the motivation comes from having tried other groups and not feeling satisfied. Many successful professionals are tired of what they call "the networking dating game" and are looking for an easy way to get together to learn and to share experiences.

> **Real life.** Jim, a marketing consultant, was invited to join a Circle two years ago, but he declined. He was in the process of "doing the circuit" and trying out a number of different networking groups. He joined a professional marketing association but soon realized that he was surrounded by his competitors. He joined a local lead-generating group and found it too stressful trying to generate the number of leads required to stay in the group. He joined a few other industry-based associations and

grew increasingly frustrated. It was only at that point that Jim decided to join a Circle.

The more motivated the members are to join, the more energy they will bring to the Circle. Some members start somewhat reserved but warm up over time. The ideal member is one who is keen to join.

In an ideal group each of the members' individual reasons for joining would overlap. The reasons would never be identical, nor would you want them to be, but you do want to be sure that everyone's goals for the Circle are similar.

> **Real life.** I met with one group of women who were interested in setting up a Circle of women leaders. We sat in a circle and each woman introduced herself and described how she saw herself as a woman and a leader. The last woman to speak said that she did not really see herself as a leader. She explained that she had not experienced much of what the other women had experienced, such as the glass ceiling. She felt so much "greener" than the rest and questioned whether she "fit" in this particular Circle. This woman decided to join a different Circle that included more people at her particular stage.

Stage of life, business or career

Another factor to consider when inviting members is the stage at which they are at. This stage can be thought of in terms of either life, business or career or a combination of all three. You will want to select members who are at similar but not necessarily identical stages.

Each person develops at his or her own pace over a lifetime. Although these changes are often linked to age, this is not always the case. In her book *New Passages,* Gail Sheehy describes the following life stages:

- Tryout Twenties

- Turbulent Thirties

- Flourishing Forties

- Flaming Fifties

- Serene Sixties

Each of these stages describes not just personal and professional goals, but challenges and struggles. It describes what people value and where they focus their energies.

Although you might wish to include members from each of these stages to share the wisdom of each stage, be sure that the differences are not too large. For example, you could include members from the Flaming Fifties and Serene Sixties but not the Tryout Twenties. If you invite someone too distant from where the others are developmentally, the roles within the Circle shift and the Circle loses balance. Often the mature members tend to take on mentoring roles and begin acting like teachers rather than partners in learning.

> **Real life.** A group of lawyers formed a Circle hoping to use it to help mentor the newer members in the firm. After about three meetings they noticed that two of the newest lawyers were not speaking very much. When approached, the young lawyers emphasized that they were learning so much and simply did not feel compelled to contribute.

Although this situation might appear fine, the information and experience exchange tended to flow one way. This meant a loss in terms of learning for the senior lawyers and, more importantly, a fundamental imbalance in the Circle. In an imbalanced Circle the conversation will not be as relevant to all and the Circle will not last as long because all members will not be benefiting equally. To counter this imbalance, the group decided to invite another junior lawyer and a senior paralegal to join their Circle.

Related to stage differences are age differences. If there are significant differences in age among members, mentor-like relationships often emerge, although this can often depend on the maturity of the individuals.

Businesses also have various stages of growth, and so do careers. Each stage is reflected by a number of factors. For example, a person just setting up a business will ask quite different questions than people who have been in business twenty years or more. A person who has just begun working in a new job will be less inclined to explore career options than a person who has just left a position and wants to become a consultant.

The best mix of Circle members seems to be those who have been in business a similar length of time. For example, it works well to combine those who have been in business three to five years and those who have been in business five to ten years.

Perceived conflict or competition

One of the basic premises of a Circle is that it must be a safe place to have an authentic conversation. If, for some reason, one of the members feels that having another member there might prevent them from being candid, then it is best to have these people in two different Circles.

There are many reasons for perceived competition or a conflict of interest, such as a past relationship, a divorce or business conflict, or a competing business interest. The key is not to question the reasons behind the conflict. It does not matter if they are real or not. What matters is that each person feels completely free to share their thoughts and opinions without feeling defensive or even awkward.

Here are some examples of perceived conflict or competition:

- a manager and executive who might compete for a position
- two executive directors in the same industry
- consultants who provide similar training to similar clients
- a business owner and their supplier
- two professionals who have similar clients

Other considerations

Now that you know whom to invite, you may want to know whom *not* to invite. The following are some general guidelines.

- *Friends.* Although friends might seem like a natural option, if you bring a friend into a Circle, that friendship shifts into another type of relationship. You may want to think about whether you or your friend wants that change.

- *Acquaintances.* Acquaintances are ideal, since you know a bit about them but have not had the opportunity to get to know them better.

- *Family members.* Although there are Circles that consist of only family members, it is generally best not to include family members in a mixed Circle. This allows all members to be completely candid and avoids the perception that not all members are equal in the Circle....

- *Mixed genders.* Some Circles work better when there is only one gender. For example, some men may prefer to form a Circle of only men to discuss things that are unique to men. Some women may feel safer and more open in a group of only women. Research shows that communication shifts significantly with different gender mixes. You should pick the mix in which you feel most comfortable to share and learn.

Sample invitation script

Once you decide to set up your own Circle, here is a sample script to help you when inviting members:

> **Script:** *Hi, I am [your name] and I am pulling together a group of people to meet on a regular basis – like a peer-mentoring group or personal advisory board. In this group we would all help each other*

solve day-to-day problems and reach our goals. I would like you to be part of this group.

Can I tell you more so you can decide if you would like to join us? If not, you might know someone who would be interested.

I read a book called One Circle. *It describes the benefits of having a powerful advisory group and describes step-by-step how to set one up. In simple terms, you invite five to eight people to meet and follow a process that stimulates discussion about the things that are important to you and the group. These discussions can range from finding new employees to dealing with day-to-day problems at work and in life.*

You are one of eight people that I am approaching. My plan is to meet once a month in our boardroom after work – say, 4:00 p.m. to 6:00 p.m. Once I have invited members, we will all meet and I will explain the process in more detail.

The only thing you need to decide right now is whether you would like to join. If you do, I will send you a list of frequently asked questions and let you know the date and time of our first meeting.

Who will be the temporary Circle Guide?

The last question you need to ask when starting out is: Who will be the Circle Guide? The first Circle Guide will usually be the person who invites the members and sets up the Circle.

This person will usually be responsible for the first few meetings and specifically the following tasks:

- inviting the members
- selecting a location and date
- providing members with information on the One Circle model
- hosting the first few meetings

Chapters 6 and 7 provide detailed instructions and scripts for the first six meetings. During one of the first few meetings the group will discuss how they wish to deal with the role of the guide. They will decide who will be the guide at each meeting (internal or external) and how the role will rotate or change between members. The original guide usually stays in the role until the group is fairly well established, and at least for the first three meetings.

Getting started: A checklist

Use this checklist to record your ideas while you are getting your Circle started.

1. Why do you want a Circle? Write your personal purpose statement in the space below. Here are some examples:

    - I am an entrepreneur wanting to grow my business.
    - I am an executive wanting to become a better leader.
    - I am a manager wanting to mentor others.
    - I am a professional wanting to grow personally and professionally.

- I am a parent wanting to be a better caregiver.
- I am a person looking for a new career.

_____

_____

2. Where will you meet? List possibilities here:
   - member's home
   - boardroom
   - quiet restaurant
   - community center
   - other _____

   _____

   _____

   _____

3. How long will you meet?
   - 1 hour
   - 1.5 hours
   - 2 hours
   - 2.5 hours
   - 3 hours
   - other _____

4. How often will you meet?
   - once a week
   - every two weeks
   - every three weeks
   - once a month

5. How long will the Circle last?
    - six months
    - one year
    - two years
    - indefinitely
    - other _____

6. When will you meet?
    - early in the morning at _____ a.m.
    - over lunchtime at _____ p.m.
    - immediately after work at _____ p.m.
    - in the evening at _____ p.m.
    - other _____

7. Whom will you invite? List names here:

    _____

    _____

    _____

8. Who will be the temporary Circle Guide? List options here:

    _____

    _____

    _____

Once you have established logistics you can schedule your first meeting. At that meeting you will begin applying the Circle Principles and Circle Process that are described in the next two chapters.

Chapter 4

························

One Circle Practices

Circles are ancient spaces, recurring in various forms in many cultures. Probably our ancestors gathered in a circle around a fire, just as families gather around the kitchen table today. Circles provide spaces where this deeper connecting can happen – where conflicts become opportunities for building relationships.

—Kay Pranis et al., *Peacemaking Circles*

Certain practices or skills encourage conversations. As people become better at these practices, they increase their chances of having more meaningful conversations. These practices are particularly important in Circles, since the focus of each Circle is on conversations.

The four Circle Practices are as follows: intention, speaking, listening and guiding. This chapter describes each of these practices in detail and provides instruction on how to practice these in Circles. Also included is an explanation of how most

Circles evolve over time – from members getting to know each other to parting ways. At the end of this chapter is a summary of the four Circle Practices for easy reference.

Circle Practices are skills in action. They can be developed over time and with practice. Although most people have some ability in each of these skills, the ways in which these skills are exercised in the Circle are somewhat unique. The extent to which members apply these skills impacts not only the richness of the conversation but also the sense of safety within the Circle – and ultimately the success of the Circle. If members remain unskilled, the Circle will suffer.

The following example demonstrates how lack of skill in the practices can impact a meeting.

> **Real life.** I was invited to speak to a group of business owners over a casual lunch. These executives all knew each other very well and had been meeting together regularly for months. During my presentation, two men started chatting to each other. I stopped and waited for them to finish. A few minutes later they began again. I stopped again. One of the men then said to me, "Oh, don't stop on our account. We are talking about something else." After the meeting, the host of the meeting apologized profusely and told me that these two men did this all the time. I then said to him: "And what do you and the others in the group do about this?"

The group in this example had several people with underdeveloped skills. Most obviously, the two chatting men lacked listening skills, but equally important, the other people around the table lacked assertiveness skills. Although each person noticed the interruption, no one intervened. This suggests either that the other members were not bothered by the interruption, did not consider it their responsibility to act or did not know how to stop it properly. With better communication skills, they probably would have acted differently.

Besides listening and speaking skills, another skill that could have been more developed in this group was the guiding skill, as practiced by the organizer of the meeting. If the host had been more skilled, he could have prevented the speaker from having to interrupt her talk twice and could have ensured that the other members were not frustrated by the interruption. Most important, however, is the fact that no one did anything. This is what distinguishes a powerful group from a powerless group – a regular team from a Circle.

Practice 1. Intention

The most important Circle Practice is intention. This is the intent each person brings to the Circle, which is reflected in every action a person takes. Underlying every act is an intent or reason for the action. The only unintentional acts are impulses or habits, which happen in an almost automatic fashion.

Intentions make each act have meaning. For example, if someone says they are sorry but they are really still angry, the words will not be perceived as a real apology. The same word can mean a completely different thing when used with a different intention. This is reflected in the saying "It's not *what* you say, but *how* you say it that matters."

The intention that must be brought to each Circle consists of two parts – curiosity and compassion.

Curiosity

Margaret Wheatley, in her book *Turning to One Another,* describes curiosity as one of the fundamental principles of conversation. This curiosity is somewhat like the concept of *beginner's mind* as reflected in Buddhist philosophy. A beginner's mind is the mindset that a person has when they experience something for the very first time. It is a sense of wonder and curiosity but rarely one of judgment. As stated by Andrews in her book *The Circle of Simplicity,* "Instead of thinking of a conversation as a contest or battle, think of it as a barn-raising, something that you are all working on together. As others speak, try to suppress the instinct to criticize or compare."[1]

Compassion

The second aspect of intention is compassion. Some people believe that there are only two fundamental human intents: love and fear. Love causes people to act in a compassionate way, and fear causes people to act in a defensive way. Most actions can be seen as originating from a place of fear or a place of love.

Traditional circle teachers suggest that members must value each member as interconnected. Each person must show compassion to others in the way they would to a family member or relation. In Western society, where inequality, competition and individualism are part of daily life, this sense of connectedness must be reinforced through compassion in a Circle. In her book *Circle Works,* Fyre Graveline explains how Circles create an atmosphere of compassion and connection, what she calls "the building block of community":

[The] Circle process can teach us the foundations upon which a proper relationship to oneself and others is developed. The state of conscious awareness contained within a Circle of interconnectedness can generate openness that is rare in Western society today.[2]

Ways to practice intention

As stated, the practice of intention consists of two parts – curiosity and compassion. Here are some ways in which intention can be practiced in a Circle:

- Stay curious.
- Be open-minded.
- Be positive.
- Be supportive.
- Assume others are acting with good intent.
- Be solution oriented.
- Show mutual respect.
- Do not put others down.
- Avoid criticism.

Practice 2. Speaking

Since so much time in the Circle is spent speaking, this skill is extraordinarily valuable to the success of a Circle. As members improve their speaking skills, the Circle will be enhanced enormously.

The atmosphere in the Circle is generated to a large extent through what is said. Speaking can stimulate or dampen conversation. It can make a Circle safe or not so safe. Speaking can be seen as supportive or hostile. And we can all feel the difference. The practice of speaking involves speaking openly, speaking with respect and speaking from your own perspective.

Speaking openly

Speaking openly means talking with honesty and from the heart as well as from the head. It means speaking in a candid yet kind way. Each person must come to the Circle with the intent to communicate openly. The quality of the conversations depends on the candor of the members. Those who possess a willingness to share the things that concern them, both personally and professionally, have a heightened opportunity to grow and learn. Andrews, in her book *The Circle of Simplicity,* urges people to speak with the emotion they feel:

> We spend a lot of our lives trying to look successful: acting as if our families have no problems, that we love our work, that we know what we're doing. No one really gets to know us .... so we must strive to be real, to be as authentic as possible. So speak with the emotion you feel. Don't censor yourself, don't try to sound intelligent, don't try to sound sophisticated, don't pretend to know something you don't. Take the risk of telling the truth, doing it with kindness and respect. Once you realize you aren't in a contest, this authenticity comes easily.[3]

Speaking with respect

Speaking with respect involves speaking in a way that takes into consideration the other person. It involves speaking in a way that does not offend and that encourages others to feel welcome. It involves adjusting what you say or how you say it to ensure the people receiving it are not offended or hurt.

In order to speak with respect, you must understand the potential impact of your speaking on others. By recognizing this impact, each person can practice showing respect in different situations and contexts. The following describes how people tend to react in certain situations. This will help you begin to understand how others feel, thus helping you better demonstrate respect and perhaps empathy.

- Those who feel they are being attacked will often go silent or, in contrast, will lash out verbally.

- Silence is often uncomfortable, and some people to try to fill this void with conversation.

- Those who feel repeatedly interrupted or confronted will often stop contributing.

- People will not always show that they are hurt, frustrated or angry.

- Many people are embarrassed by displays of emotion so try to control such outbursts.

The most important thing to recognize is that not everyone will react in the same way, on the same day, in a similar situation. Before speaking, it is helpful to ask yourself the following questions:

- What do I want to say?

- Why am I saying it?

- How does it relate to what is being said?

- How will the group or individual interpret it?

- What are some likely impacts to what I might say?

These questions are not designed to cause you to edit what you say as much as to help you understand why you are speaking and to take responsibility for the consequences of your speaking. Each person should be conscious of their words and their potential impact.

Speaking from your own perspective

The third aspect of the One Circle Practice of speaking is speaking from your own perspective. This means describing exactly what happened, how you perceived events and how you were impacted. If ever in doubt about how to speak, it is always best to simply tell your story. The amazing thing about speaking about our own experiences is that they are simply that: our own perspective. No one can take away from what you saw or what you felt. It is your story – true or not.

The importance of speaking from your own perspective is best demonstrated in situations of conflict. If you describe how you were impacted by another person's actions, without blaming, the other person will be more willing to listen and to resolve the conflict. A useful conflict resolution technique applies this practice by using "I" statements rather than "you" statements.

Read and compare the following pairs of statements and ask yourself: Which ones open up the conversation and which ones shut down the conversation?

- When you interrupted me **I** felt you were not listening to me.

- **You** were wrong to interrupt me!

- You talked on and on and therefore **you** don't respect me.

- When you showed up late **I** felt like you did not value me or my time.

- **You** are always late and **you** never say sorry.

Notice that the "you" statements tend to blame and judge, whereas the "I" statements tend to describe the perspective of the person being impacted. Rather than blaming, they describe the impact that the other person's actions had on them. The person receiving the message is thus less likely to go on the defensive. Besides using "I" statements, three other helpful communication practices are asking questions, paraphrasing and summarizing.

In a Circle, the more questions the better. As stated by Naguib Mahfouz, "You can tell whether a man is clever by his answer. You can tell whether a man is wise by his questions." The ideal questions are open-ended. These are questions that cannot be answered with a yes or no. They invite elaboration and require the speaker to talk more about the situation. This enables the group to better understand what is being said. Here are some examples:

- Tell us more.

- What are your thoughts on that?

- How did that make you feel?

- I wonder what might happen if Don did that?

When asking questions it is important to inquire from a genuine desire to understand and not to critique or criticize. Any challenges in the form of questions must be posed with the intent to bring clarity as opposed to shut down the conversation.

Two other useful speaking skills are paraphrasing and summarizing. Paraphrasing involves repeating back what you heard but in different words. Here are two examples of paraphrasing:

- "I think I heard you say that .... Is that what you are suggesting?"

- "So what you are saying is .... Is that correct?"

By paraphrasing you demonstrate that you understood what was being said and at the same time allow the speaker to clarify the original message.

Summarizing, on the other hand, is just that: summarizing what was said. Summarizing is useful for pulling together several ideas or for bringing closure to a long conversation. The risk with summarizing is that it can be perceived as taking liberties with another person's words or as a way of shutting down the conversation. Therefore, it should be used with care.

Ways to practice speaking

As stated, the practice of speaking involves speaking openly, speaking with respect and speaking from your own perspective. Here are ways in which speaking can be practiced in a Circle:

- Speak openly.
- Speak candidly, with kindness.
- Speak with respect.
- Reflect before speaking.
- Be aware of whether and how others are speaking.
- Use "I" statements rather than "you" statements.
- Describe your experiences through stories.
- Ask questions.
- Paraphrase and summarize.

No one is a perfect communicator, and it is the responsibility of each member of the group to commit to becoming a better communicator, not only by listening better but by providing constructive feedback and being able to describe their own needs and perspectives in a way that enhances communication.

Practice 3. Listening

Another essential skill associated with Circles is the skill of listening. This involves listening with your whole body, listening without judging and listening without an agenda.

When you listen you must really listen. Listen with curiosity and a desire to understand. Listen with your ears, your eyes and all your senses. To listen effectively you must listen to the words as well as the underlying meaning. You must listen to what is being said and what is not being said. It is also helpful to maintain eye contact and watch body language, especially facial expressions.

Listening means hearing without judging. It does not matter whether you agree or disagree with another member of the Circle. All that matters is that you listen and accept that each person will have different experiences and opinions. It is best to listen to others' experiences without making conclusions. They are neither right nor wrong; they simply are.

The practice of listening also means listening without an agenda. If you are thinking ahead, you are likely not listening. If you are planning what you want to say, you are not really listening. If you are thinking about your response before it is your turn to speak you are not only not listening, but you are disrupting the natural evolution of the dialogue in the Circle. Sometimes it helps to keep in mind that your role in the Circle is not to solve the problems of other members but rather to allow the solution to rise to the surface.

Listening is difficult for many people because they want to control or direct the conversation. They like to anticipate where the conversation might lead and insert their ideas at the appropriate time. This, unfortunately, does not allow the conversation to unfold naturally. It does not allow it to weave and meander and find a solution along its natural course. People tend not to trust the conversation and are uncomfortable knowing its direction. Unexpected turns, however, often uncover hidden solutions and allow for breakthrough thinking. In our fast-paced society, it takes practice to simply let go of our thoughts and remain open.

Ways to practice listening

As described, the practice of listening involves listening with your whole body, listening without judging and listening without an agenda. Here are ways in which listening can be practiced in a Circle:

- Listen with curiosity.
- Listen with a desire to understand.
- Listen with your mind and body.
- Maintain eye contact.
- Watch body language.
- Watch facial expressions.
- Listen without judging.
- Listen without a plan or agenda.
- Let people speak without interruption.

Practice 4. Guiding

The fourth Circle Practice is guiding. Since all members of the Circle are responsible for the functioning of the Circle and will usually assume the role of Circle Guide at some point, the skill of guiding is particularly important. This practice involves hosting the meetings, modeling the Circle Practices and facilitating conversations when necessary.

Hosting

The skill of guiding is much like the skill of hosting. The Circle Guide's responsibility is to ensure that the Circle functions properly and the members benefit. The guide selects the date and location of the meeting, invites the members and hosts the meeting.

During the Circle meeting the guide's main role is to protect the Circle Principles, Practices and Process. But recall that all of the members share this role, so the guide's main role is mostly to lead the group through the Circle Process, from preparation to closing. This includes setting up the space, bringing the necessary equipment, keeping track of time and ensuring that each member has had an opportunity to contribute.

Although it may not seem like much, the role of Circle Guide is critical to the Circle. The guide helps support the feeling of safety by offering predictability in applying the Circle Process. Members appreciate knowing what to expect. By meetings following a consistent process, each member will grow more comfortable in the Circle.

Modeling

The guide should model the Circle Practices and particularly those of appropriate listening and speaking. The guide should see this role as a great honor and great responsibility. An honorable guide would never abuse her power and as described here:

> She realizes her position of leadership is a great honor but also a great responsibility and she takes this responsibility very seriously. She understands

she is a role model and because of this, she has a great deal of influence on others even as she consciously works on remaining humble. Certainly she does not take advantage of this position of power by manipulating, coercing or gaining favors from those who hold her in esteem.[4]

To be good, a Circle Guide must be alert, adaptable and honest. If the guide does not know how to proceed, it is best if they say so. If they are trying something new, they should let the others know. The guide must trust the resources of the group and tap into their energy to create synergies. The guide must also have a sense of humor. Things will not always run smoothly, and this is okay.

Facilitating

The Circle Guide will start the Circle, watch and listen, monitor the energy level, watch the contribution of each member and intervene only when absolutely necessary. Only rarely will Circles require facilitation, and when they do they tend to need short interventions such as prompting or redirecting conversations. Silence is perhaps the most powerful tool and, as a general rule, saying less is better.

A Circle Guide can on occasion enhance a conversation if it seems to be floundering, if members are not participating or if members are participating too much. For example, if a member is daydreaming or zoning out, the guide can call for a break. Only rarely will the guide be called on to resolve a conflict. Although each member is responsible for easing tension, if this does not occur naturally, then the guide must intervene. Here are some examples of the type of language a skilled guide might use in a difficult situation:

- "I see that we are at a bit of a deadlock. I suggest we move things forward. I would like each of you to reflect for thirty seconds, and then I would like to hear one sentence from each of you as to how we can move on."

- "I would like to hear what others have to say. Jim and Steve have had enough time to voice their concerns. I will dedicate the next five minutes to others."

- "I am not sure we will resolve this today. I would like us to go away and think about it and come back to the next Circle to discuss it. Could I hear what others think?"

The guide should be particularly aware of his or her tone when speaking. There is a fine balance being assertive, respectful and inclusive.

A few words need to be said about emotions. Many people are uncomfortable with emotions – not just those of others, but also their own. They are often afraid that they or others will be embarrassed by a show of emotions.

Emotions have gotten a bad rap over the past few centuries. Because they are not rational, they have historically been viewed as dangerous and destructive. Luckily, recent research has demonstrated the value and importance of emotions. Not only are emotions healthy, but they are critical to such basic functions as thinking and decision making.

Emotions are also the key to our intuition and our deeper sense of knowing. They give us insight to the hidden feelings and thoughts that might be preventing us from moving ahead. To exclude emotions from a conversation is not only impossible, but could be detrimental. Emotions are normal and should be allowed to surface in a natural way.

Feelings should not be labeled as good or bad, but rather as a natural response to an event.

Ways to practice guiding

As described, the practice of guiding involves hosting the meetings, modeling the Circle Practices and facilitating conversations if necessary. Here are ways in which guiding can be practiced in a Circle:

- Guide the Circle Process.
- Protect the Circle Principles.
- Be consistent.
- Model the Circle Practices.
- Be alert, adaptable and honest.
- Appreciate emotions.
- Watch and listen.
- Ask open-ended questions and use silence.
- Monitor the energy level.

The evolution of a Circle

Every Circle will evolve over time. It will usually start slowly and then experience bursts of growth. By understanding the typical evolution of a Circle, you will be more accepting of the ups and downs that come with being in a group. You may also be able to shift your own attitudes and behaviors to allow for the group and its members to evolve naturally.

Recent research on groups suggests that most will go through a number of stages in their development. One of the more common models of team development describes the stages as norming, forming, conforming and storming.

Like any group, a Circle will go through a number of stages as it grows. Not every group will experience these stages, but by understanding them you may better see what might be happening as your Circle grows. For example, knowing that your group will struggle at some point enables you to remain committed when things get a bit rough. You will understand what is happening and may be more inclined to work through the issues. Here are the typical stages of Circle evolution.

Stage 1. Connection – Getting to know each other

The first stage of a Circle is called Connection. At this stage the group begins to form a loose connection, and the members spend most of their time getting acquainted. People are generally agreeable and tentatively share opinions but, because they do not know each other well, they tend to be a bit reserved. They might be curious about what will happen but they are also cautious and a bit skeptical, since they have not developed much trust. However, at the start members tend to be pleasant, are cooperative and tend to get along quite well.

At this stage it is important to understand that you cannot create an instant relationship. Intimacy or even acceptance of others is simply not possible. There is minimal self-disclosure, and differences are simply ignored. Genuine deep conversation is unlikely to occur. This is okay. Do not rush.

To help break down this initial discomfort, it is useful to use ice-breaker exercises. These are short activities that help members get to know each other better. They are effective at getting conversations started. Many Circles start the conversation by having a general conversation about how they heard about Circles and what they hope to get out of a Circle.

Since one of the main functions of a Circle is to build strong relationships, the process of the Circle is deliberately paced to allow for bonds to grow somewhat naturally, in an unforced way. The first few meetings are usually dedicated to getting to know each other better and clarifying expectations.

The group often reaches a turning point after a few meetings, and members become ready to make a formal commitment to each other and the group itself. Some groups hold a commitment ritual or make a symbolic act during this stage, to demonstrate their commitment to the Circle. This is described here:

> When all members feel strongly about their bond, they may wish to hold a simple commitment ritual, consisting of a symbolic act and a statement. Each person might light a candle, or place a valued object into a cloth to form the group's "medicine bundle." Such a ritual serves to remind each person of the group's connection to their lives. Every person clearly states just what it is he or she is committing to, for example, a set of values, attendance at meetings, confidentiality, and/or a vision for the future.[5]

Near the end of this stage, the Circle achieves a fairly high level of group confidence. This emerges as each of the members opens up and begins to share their hopes and dreams. Members will begin to feel a sense of belonging and will truly enjoy attending the Circle. They will have developed the necessary trust to begin to have more meaningful conversations.

Stage 2. Conflict – Having candid conversations

The second stage in the development of a Circle is called Conflict. At this stage members begin to have more candid conversations and in doing so disclose feelings and opinions. At this stage the group will either grow deeper or fall apart. During this stage, members are not as polite as they were previously, and differences tend to surface. This stage is described as follows:

> In stage two, not only are the differences in opinions, views, attitudes, and feelings put on the table, the differences are the main event. This is a stage of struggle and fighting. Usually, we are so uncomfortable with other people viewing life differently that we make it our mission to change them. We assume they must be fixed, and we go about it ardently. The discussions will sound like battles of will, and they are. This is a power struggle: Who is right? Who will prevail?[6]

Members may feel unhappy or frustrated and may feel a loss of connection or commitment at this stage. Polarization can occur and, if not addressed in a constructive way, can be fairly disruptive and damaging. Even silence can cause a group to shut down.

When members realize they are at this stage, they can better recognize what is going on and learn to appreciate it as a natural evolution rather than a serious dysfunction. By using proper communication skills and showing openness and respect, Circles can move through all sorts of differences. It is important to remember that a diverse group is often most functional and useful. Although each person might like the comfort of being surrounded by others like themselves, if members are too similar, they will not challenge you to be your best.

Stage 3. Creation – Building and collaborating

The third stage, called Creation, involves building and collaborating. At this stage the group moves past their individual differences and develops a deep sense of connectedness. The kind of conversations that emerge are of a caliber that could never be achieved in the prior two stages. Members treat each others as close colleagues and speak with an intent that is more genuine and supportive. Author Scott Peck calls this stage "emptiness," because it consists of emptying ourselves of the beliefs and assumptions that prevent us from really hearing the other members. At this stage the Circle often acknowledges the successes of the members and of the Circle and finds many occasions to celebrate. At this stage members feel reconnected, empowered and excited.

Parting ways

There may also be an ending stage, when you decide to dismantle your Circle or part ways. You may all agree that you have accomplished all you wanted to accomplish. You may wish to leave a Circle or form another Circle with different people. This should not be seen as a negative, but rather as a natural evolution. It is rare for a Circle to last forever, and part of its maturing is when members recognize the Circle is declining in usefulness. How to deal with one member's departure is covered in chapter 8.

Summary of Circle Practices

Here is a summary of the ways members can practice the four Circle Practices.

Intention

The practice of intention consists of two parts – curiosity and compassion. Intention can be practiced in a Circle in the following ways:

- Stay curious.

- Be open-minded.

- Be positive.

- Be supportive.

- Assume others are acting with good intent.

- Be solution oriented.

- Show mutual respect.

- Do not put others down.

- Avoid criticism.

Speaking

The practice of speaking involves speaking openly, speaking with respect and speaking from your own perspective. Here are ways in which speaking can be practiced in a Circle:

- Speak openly.
- Speak candidly, with kindness.
- Speak with respect.
- Reflect before speaking.
- Be aware of whether and how others are speaking.
- Use "I" statements rather than "you" statements.
- Describe your experiences through stories.
- Ask questions.
- Paraphrase and summarize.

Listening

The practice of listening involves listening with your whole body, listening without judging and listening without an agenda. Here are ways in which listening can be practiced in a Circle:

- Listen with curiosity.
- Listen with a desire to understand.
- Listen with your mind and body.
- Maintain eye contact.

- Watch body language.

- Watch facial expressions.

- Listen without judging.

- Listen without a plan or agenda.

- Let people speak without interruption.

Guiding

The practice of guiding involves hosting the meetings, modeling the Circle Practices and facilitating conversations if necessary. Ways in which guiding can be practiced in a Circle include the following:

- Guide the Circle Process.

- Protect the Circle Principles.

- Be consistent.

- Model the Circle Practices.

- Be alert, adaptable and honest.

- Appreciate emotions.

- Watch and listen.

- Ask open-ended questions and use silence.

- Monitor the energy level.

When these One Circle Practices are used during Circle meetings, the conversation tends to flow more easily and individuals tend to feel heard. Over time and with practice, members get more proficient at these skills and are able to use them both within and outside the Circle. The next chapter describes the One Circle Process – the last of the three fundamental parts of the One Circle model.

The circle challenges us to break out of our assumed helplessness and look, again and again, for the points of empowerment where we can fulfill our own (and other people's) needs, accomplish purpose, and take a stand.

—Christina Baldwin, *Calling the Circle*

Chapter 5

....

The One Circle
Process

T he main objective when conducting a Circle is to encourage the participation of each of the members.
When members participate, the conversation flows. Each person leaves with a sense of having contributed and a sense of
completeness. When members do not participate, the conversation feels awkward and stifled. Members leave with an
uncomfortable, dissatisfied feeling.

The One Circle process encourages participation in
three ways: by adopting the One Circle Principles, by committing to the One Circle Practices and by following the One
Circle Process. This chapter describes the One Circle Process
step by step, including the role of the Circle Guide and the use
of rituals.

Each Circle meeting has a beginning, middle and end.
Each person is invited into the Circle and enters the Circle
with the intention to engage in conversation. The authors
of *Wisdom Circles* talk about the concept of *temenos* – or a
sacred container. The Circle becomes the container for the

conversation, like a cup or chalice. The Circle contains the conversation and treats it as a special place or sanctuary. The Circle Process provides the necessary structure to create a container of safety, as described here:

> In order to create a safe and supportive environment you must create a circle with a well-defined and purposeful structure. This structure, instead of feeling limiting, will actually put people at ease. We are all afraid of the unknown, and your circle structure forms the foundation from which participants can enter the unknown with some degree of comfort.[1]

The One Circle Process is designed to enable rich conversations and to enhance the longevity of the group. The process has several components that play a unique role in creating a safe and welcoming place. Each step is important and should not be rushed through or skipped. Each part is designed to set the foundation for the next. The seven parts of the Circle Process are as follows:

1. Preparing for the Circle

2. The Opening

3. The Check-In

4. Topic Selection

5. The Conversation

6. The Check-Out

7. The Closing

The Circle Guide leads the Circle Process and is responsible for making sure that the Circle runs smoothly from beginning to end. Some of the functions of a Circle Guide are to set up the Circle meeting, lead the group through the Circle Process, ensure that everyone has an opportunity to speak, keep track of time and bring forward action items. After arranging the Circle meeting and setting a time and location, the guide is ready to begin the Circle Process and prepare for the Circle meeting.

Preparing for the Circle

In preparing for the Circle, the guide will need to select a talking piece, purchase a journal, prepare an agenda and prepare the space.

Select a talking piece

The talking piece is an object that is passed around from person to person as each person speaks. Each person holds the piece while speaking. The authors of *The Way of Council* describe the importance of the talking piece:

> The talking piece represents the organizing principle of council and powerfully communicates the spirit of the circle. Its presence reminds everyone of their commitment to the form and intentions of the process. Holding the piece empowers expression. Watching it move around the circle supports attentive listening.[2]

The talking piece can be any item, such as a piece of driftwood, a coin, a bowl or any other object that might represent the group or its purpose. Here are more examples:

Objects that are frequently used as talking pieces include old Bibles or other family heirlooms, traditional and contemporary rattles, crystals, stones, shells, rain sticks, and particular ceremonial objects that honor the council location or the traditions of the group. We hasten to add that the talking piece needn't convey solemnity. Sometimes lighthearted or whimsical objects are appropriate, particularly if the circle has been taking itself too seriously.[3]

In most Circles, the original Circle Guide will select the first piece, and later the members of the group will select their own unique talking piece. Some groups use different talking pieces for different occasions.

Purchase a journal

Some groups keep a Circle journal to track the progress of the Circle. This journal belongs to the whole Circle and can, over time, become a shared history of the group. At the minimum the journal will include the names of and contact information for the members.

Typically a group will dedicate a few pages in the journal to each meeting. The Circle Guide or another person will write a few notes on those pages right after the meeting. Some of the things that can be recorded are as follows:

- who was in attendance
- what generally transpired in the Circle meeting
- accomplishments of individuals
- topics for discussion
- ways to improve the process

- items to be discussed at the next meeting
- the progress of the Circle

An easy way to ensure that something gets recorded is to designate one person to be the journal keeper at each meeting. This person would be responsible for recording anything relevant after that meeting and would pass the journal on to the next journal keeper at the next meeting.

Keeping a journal can provide continuity from meeting to meeting. It means members do not have to remember what happened at the meeting or what they will be doing at the next meeting. It is particularly useful for bringing items forward, such as suggestions for improving the process.

It is a good idea for members to bring their own journals as well. This journal can be used for their personal reflection and learning. It can also include goals, challenges and to-do lists.

Prepare an agenda

The Circle Guide must prepare an agenda. The agenda is used by the guide to help lead the Circle, from opening to closing. The agenda is pre-set in that it follows the previously listed step-by-step Circle Process:

- The Opening
- The Check-In
- Topic Selection
- The Conversation
- The Check-Out
- The Closing

It is useful when preparing an agenda to write short scripts for each part. These scripts allow the guide to stay focused on the conversation until it is time to move to the next item on the agenda. Scripts are also useful for concluding one part and opening the next part of the agenda. For example, here is a sample script for the Opening:

> **Script:** *Hello and welcome everyone. I will now open this Circle. Thank you all for coming. We have come to this Circle to engage in meaningful conversations. The purpose of this particular group is to help each other be their best at work and in life. We have each committed to the Circle Principles and Circle Practices. I will be the guide for the Circle today. I will open the Circle with a short quotation. I will then invite each of you to check in with a few words about how you feel and what you expect from today's Circle.*

Other sample scripts can be found in chapters 6 and 7.

Prepare the space

The Circle Guide must prepare the space. In her book *Circle Works*, Fyre Graveline suggests that in traditional circles, in order to honor the traditions of the Elders, the Circle space should be prepared carefully. It should be clean and orderly, with particular attention paid to lighting and air quality.

Preparing the space means selecting a place where there will be no interruptions and where all members can sit comfortably in a circle. The room must be private so that others cannot overhear the conversation. There can be chairs, pillows or benches for seating, but they must be set up in a circle.

After preparing for the Circle, the next step in the One Circle Process is the Opening.

The Opening

The Opening of the Circle sets the tone for the entire Circle so must be done with care and attention. Since the purpose of any Circle is to provide a safe place for a candid conversation, safety is a primary goal for the guide.

The Circle Guide will first ask members to sit in a circle. The seating arrangement does not matter. It is best for members to sit where they feel most comfortable, since this adds to a sense of safety. The circle must have no "head," no top point and no favored position.

Once everyone is sitting down, the guide will open the Circle and begin to create a space of calm presence. The guide may ask members to relax, breathe deeply or stretch gently and will usually say or do something that clearly marks the beginning of the Circle. This could be reciting a quotation or lighting a candle.

Before moving to the next part, the Circle Guide may want to mention any celebrations, outstanding matters, housekeeping items or issues that were raised at prior Circle meetings. After the Opening there is a brief Check-In.

The Check-In

During the Check-In members pass the talking piece around the Circle and briefly say how they are feeling and what they hope for during the Circle time. This usually takes a few minutes per person. Each speaker should not be interrupted during this time, and a talking piece can be used.

The Check-In serves three main purposes. It re-establishes the contact between members, it creates the Circle connection, and it becomes one of the main rituals. It can also bring to the surface topics for discussion. Here is sample script for the Check-In:

> **Script:** *Now that I have formally opened the Circle, we will do a check-in. I will pass around the talking piece. You will each have a few minutes to say how you are feeling and what you hope to achieve in this particular Circle. We will then select our topic of conversation.*

Topic Selection

There are two ways to select a topic for conversation. One is to select a topic before the meeting, and the other is to select a topic at the beginning of the meeting. Some groups keep a list of items for discussion and select one for each meeting. Others prefer to discuss issues that are immediately relevant.

If you decide to select a topic at the beginning of the meeting, you simply need to pass the talking piece around to seek ideas. You can either ask for ideas directly or ask reflective-type questions that will uncover relevant issues.

An easy way to uncover topics is by asking the same question at the beginning of every meeting. This question will help individuals identify their own issues and concerns. It also makes choosing a topic fairly quick, because members anticipate the question and think about it beforehand. Asking the same question provides some predictability.

Here are some reflective questions that can be asked around the Circle. It is best to pick only one.

- What was your business high and low this month?

- What was your career high and low this month?

- What was your personal high and low this month?

- Can you name one of your business goals and one recent obstacle?

- What is your career goal and one recent obstacle?

- What is your personal goal and one recent obstacle?

You will note that each question has two parts – a positive and a negative. This prevents people from talking about only positives or negatives. If you decide to use this type of question, it is best to ask each member to think about the question for a few moments before the Circle begins. Some individuals write their thoughts in their personal journals.

In most Circles several topics arise. In these situations the guide can either allow the discussion to cover all the topics generally or can focus the discussion on one or two topics. Here is a sample script:

> **Script:** *It sounds like we have a couple of choices for our topic today. We can simply have a general discussion about the topics that have come up or we can select a few specific topics for discussion. We might have time to discuss several topics. We all heard that Jennifer needs help finding a new assistant, since her current assistant left yesterday with no notice. We also heard that Jim is struggling with a current client.*

*I will pass the talking piece around. Please tell me
what you would like to discuss in this Circle and we
can quickly decide together.*

Another alternative is to have the Circle Guide select a
topic for discussion. This should be done only when ideas are
not forthcoming. The guide can either think of a brand-new
topic or bring forward ideas identified in prior meetings. It is
useful to keep a running list of topics for discussion and
update it periodically. The topics that are selected become the
focal point of the substantive part of the Circle meeting – the
Conversation.

The Conversation

The Conversation phase of the Circle Process usually lasts
over an hour and can take different forms, depending on the
group and the topic(s) of conversation. After selecting the
topic, the guide will ask the group to select a method of conversation. The three main methods are the talking piece
method, the brainstorming method and the decision-making
method. The three methods can be combined or used in
sequence.

The talking piece method

The talking piece method is the easiest and most common
method to use in Circles. The Circle Guide simply describes
the selected topic and then passes the talking piece around the
Circle. Members can speak or pass the piece on to the next
person. The talking piece is passed around and around until

the topic is exhausted. The final round is usually dedicated to tying up threads, summarizing learning or deciding on steps to move forward.

Each person is usually allowed to speak without interruption for a few minutes. Some Circles allocate specific time limits for the whole conversation or for each individual. Some Circles use a timer to ensure compliance. The key is to ensure that everyone has the amount of time they need, without feeling rushed. Each topic and each person will be different. The members can choose to remain silent, as reflected in the following comment:

> Every member of the circle always has the option of holding the talking piece in silence for a moment,... or offering a simple gesture, and/or passing it on without speaking. Silence may be appropriate when there is no inner indication of a need for expression or if one prefers to hear more of the other voices before speaking during a subsequent round.[4]

Although there are no rules about what can be said, the general idea is for each person to share a situation or experience with the group. The easiest way to begin is by telling stories. For example, you might talk about a similar situation that happened to you or about an article you read on the topic. Each member will have different experiences and opinions, and all contribute to make the Circle rich.

Each person will speak for themselves from their own perspective. Although members may build upon what another member has said, it is best to simply focus on what can be added. It is good practice to avoid giving direct advice, particularly before an issue has been discussed in any detail. Often the original issue is not the most important issue. Other problems may surface and disclose the real causes of a problem. This is part of the synergy of the Circle.

As for feedback to others, all comments directed at another person must be done with extraordinary care. Even positive or constructive feedback to provide support or advice must be done with caution. If misinterpreted, these comments can cause the conversation to slow. Any comments about what another person has said have the potential to take away from the power of the speaker's message. Simple silence often provides enough acknowledgment.

The talking piece can be passed to members across the circle or can be passed in one direction. The random passing of the piece allows for fairly free flow of thoughts and emotions. The conversation takes the shape of a true dialogue. The one-direction pass tends to keep emotions under control and encourage more reasoned thinking, as described here:

> The talking piece helps to manage the discussion of very emotional issues. Emotions can be expressed without the emotions taking over the dialogue. Because participants must wait for the talking piece to speak they cannot respond without thinking. Because the talking piece must go around the circle, it prevents two individuals from getting into a back-and-forth emotional exchange. If the words of one participant anger another, multiple members of the circle may address the issues raised before the talking piece reaches the angry participant, thus relieving the angry participant from a sense of needing to defend him/herself alone.[5]

When passing the piece in one direction, be sure to decide who will speak first and the order of speaking. The simplest way is to pass the piece around the circle in a clockwise direction. According to the authors of *The Way of Council,* this is the "sun" direction used in most traditional councils.

> I have often imagined that the circle is a loom and the talking piece a shuttle that moves around it, weaving the threads of the people's stories together in unpredictable ways. The resulting tapestry may be obscure at first, but if the magic of council is awakened, its design will eventually become clear to many in the circle.[6]

The brainstorming method

Another method of conversation is brainstorming. This is useful in situations where one person has an issue and would benefit from a quick creative idea-generating session. The guide asks one member in advance to record the ideas, then asks the member with the problem to briefly describe their situation. This description should take five to ten minutes and can be timed if necessary.

The guide then opens up the Circle for questions, comments and ideas. At this point the original member remains silent, even if asked a question. This is important, because this is a time for the free flow of creative ideas. These ideas should not be stalled or stopped by comments such as "I tried that" or "I am not sure that would work because..." During this time, all suggestions are simply recorded and not judged. Once the brainstorming winds down, the list of ideas is handed back to the person who presented the problem.

Usually the member will take the list away and report back at the next meeting. This avoids the entire meeting being taken up canvassing the pros and cons of each suggestion. The person with the problem may bring the item back to the group for further discussion and help, but it will be considered as a topic at the beginning of the meeting in the same way that other topics are considered.

The decision-making method

A third method of conversation is the decision-making method. This method is used when one or several members in combination want to come to a decision on some issue. This can be on Circle-related items such as inviting a new member to the Circle or items not related to the Circle, such as whether a member should take a new job. The decision-making method has the following five parts.

1. *Describe the situation.* The person who is most concerned about an issue describes their situation for five to ten minutes, then places the talking piece in the center of the circle. Those who wish to speak pick up the talking piece and then return it to the center when done.

2. *Ask questions and reframe.* The other members ask questions and help reframe the issues. These questions are to help clarify the issue and to help the member see the situation from different perspectives. Often questions can help identify hidden blocks and feelings that are at the root of the problem.

3. *Describe the ideal state.* After exhausting questions, the member is asked one final question: What is your ideal situation?

4. *Canvass solutions.* Once the group is clear about the issue and has an idea about the ideal state, the group can then canvass solutions. This involves members brainstorming solutions. During this time, the person with the issue does not respond. One person records the solutions on a piece of paper and gives them to the member at the end of the session. The solutions are not considered in any detail at this point.

5. *Identify action steps.* The group then has the member identify about three action steps that emerged from the conversation. At the next meeting that person can report back on those action steps.

The guide must direct the group through each part of the decision-making method. Here is a sample opening script:

Script: *Kate has a situation that she needs help with. We have decided that the decision-making method is most appropriate for this conversation. As you know, this method has five steps. Kate has about five minutes to describe the situation. We will then spend about ten minutes asking Kate questions. Questions and responses should be kept to one or two sentences. These questions are to help us better understand the situation and to provide Kate with a number of perspectives. Kate will then be asked to describe her ideal situation. Armed with this picture, we will canvass solutions, without interruption. After* *solutions have been thoroughly canvassed, we will help Kate create an action plan. Any questions? Kate, please describe your situation.*

One of the most important aspects of the decision-making model is the asking of questions. Good questions will challenge assumptions, generate new ideas, uncover feelings and interests, and cause breakthrough thinking. These types of questions are unpresumptuous and come from a curiosity and a desire to clarify the situation.

As mentioned previously, open-ended questions are ideal. Here are some examples of these types of questions:

- Tell me more about ...
- What happened then?
- Could you explain further about ...?
- Who else was impacted?
- Why is this so important to you?
- What are some of the consequences of your actions?
- What resources did you use?
- How have you tried to solve the problem?
- What will happen if you do not do anything?
- What are the benefits if the problem is resolved?

How to select a method

I've outlined three forms that conversation can take in a Circle: talking piece, brainstorming and decision-making. As you can see, the method of conversation you choose depends on a number of factors and specifically on the issue to be resolved, the outcome that is expected and the preference of the group. For example, if the topic of conversation is about finding an assistant, all three methods would work. The members could pass the talking piece around the Circle and share experiences, they could brainstorm and compile a list of possible solutions, or they could use the decision-making method to identify specific steps needed to find an assistant. The final choice of method is often left to the person raising the issue and usually depends on what that person wants in terms of an outcome.

Generally speaking, if the topic is relevant to only one member, the decision-making method is best, since it can help an individual diagnose their problem and identify steps to solving the problem. If the problem is fairly straightforward and could be solved by quickly identifying solutions, the brainstorming method is best. If the topic is vague, complex or emotional, the talking piece method is best because it allows for sharing of rich personal experiences. Once you have tried each method you will get a better sense of the situations that are most appropriate for each.

Concluding the conversation

Regardless of the method selected, the conversation must be brought to a conclusion. The conclusion to brainstorming is usually a written list of ideas or solutions. The conclusion of the decision-making method of conversation is an action plan.

The conclusion of a talking piece conversation is not so obvious. This type of conversation may have no identifiable outcome. In most situations, the group will gain clarity about a problem and identify ideas about how to deal with an issue. In some situations the group will come to a consensus about a topic or identify some steps to be taken as a result of the conversation. To provide some completion to the conversation, the Circle Guide may wish to summarize the conversation. Another way to conclude is by passing around the talking piece and having each member provide their own summary or final thoughts. This provides a sense of ending to the conversation. These ideas can be captured in members' individual journals or in the Circle journal.

The Check-Out

After the Conversation there is a brief Check-Out. Usually the Circle Guide mentions that the time for closing is approaching and then invites the members to check out. In a process similar to the Check-In, the members pass the talking piece around the Circle and briefly say how they are feeling and one thing they learned during the Circle. Each person will speak for a few minutes and should not be interrupted. As with the Check-In, the guide may want to allow some quiet time before the Check-Out to allow members of the Circle to collect their thoughts, perhaps by writing in their journals.

As part of the Check-Out the guide may want to briefly review what transpired, acknowledge everyone's contribution, or mention some important breakthroughs. At this point it is also useful to identify any outstanding items and to canvass ideas for improving the Circle process. The guide can pass the talking piece around and ask for comments. Here is a sample script:

Script: *This has been a very productive Circle meeting. I get the sense that we have learned a lot about how to solve many of the problems we are confronting on a day-to-day basis. I know Jan and Barry have some specific ideas about how to move ahead. Before closing the Circle I would like to pass the talking piece around one last time to find out if there are any outstanding issues and any ideas about ways to improve the Circle process. If we do not have time to discuss these issues today, I will bring them back at the beginning of the next meeting. Kim, do you want to start?*

The guide can either facilitate a brief discussion or record the comments for a later discussion. If time is running out and there is general agreement that the items can wait until the next meeting, it is best to hold them over for discussion at the next meeting, when everyone is fresh.

The Closing

The Closing is an important aspect of the Circle and should not be rushed or, worse yet, skipped. The Closing lasts only a few minutes. After the Check-Out the guide will call the Circle to a close. It is useful to have a closing ritual such as reading a poem or placing the talking piece back in its container. The Circle should always end on a positive note. Here is a sample script for the Closing:

Script: *I am calling this Circle to a close. Thank you all for contributing to the conversation today. I would like to close with the following quotation. [Read*

quotation] Have a great week. I am looking forward
to our next Circle.

The Circle Guide's main role at this stage is to center the
Circle and then close it so that the members can go back to
their daily activities. Ideally there should be some social time
after the Circle to permit for an adjustment back to regular
conversation. It is a good idea to share refreshments to show a
common bond at this time.

Rituals

Most Circles use rituals in a variety of ways. A ritual is any
repeated gesture or action that has a symbolic meaning. Our
lives are filled with ritual, from brushing our teeth in a certain
manner to sitting in the same place when we do a certain
activity. We are ritualistic beings, as described here:

> Our urge to ritualize, to create ceremony can be
> suppressed but not suffocated. It's in our DNA. We
> hunger for it, and we do it even when we don't real-
> ize that it is what we are doing. Rituals and cere-
> mony probably play a role in your life even if you
> aren't aware of them.[7]

Rituals are powerful tools for developing a group identity and
building bonds. You might recall some rituals from holidays,
religious ceremonies, Boy Scouts or sororities. Rituals help
make an event meaningful.

In Circles, rituals are often used to mark the opening
and closing of the Circle but can also be used for many different purposes. Many rituals arise naturally, like the sharing
of food before or after the Circle. Beverly Engel, author of

Women Circling the Earth, comments on how ritual plays an integral role in Circles:

> Ritual is an essential part of all circles and a necessary element in establishing what is called "a sacred time and place." In order to be effective, ritual needs to trigger the subconscious and let it know that something important is happening. Rituals consist of evocative words and symbolic actions that are meant to invoke a sense of sanctuary and sacredness.... A ritual also needs to tell our subconscious that we are ready to change and are in a safe place to change. Ritual sets the stage, provides the structure, gives us an emotional "kick start" to effect change.[8]

Here are some rituals you might consider introducing in your Circle.

Chime or bell. A chime or a bell is a great tool for use in shifting from one time in space to another. It can be used to mark the Opening and Closing as well as different phases of the Circle. It can be used to mark the beginning or the end of a particularly difficult conversation. It reminds us of the safety of the space and the confidentiality of what is discussed.

Poem or quotation. A simple ritual involves reading a poem or quotation. The words can shift our thinking into a more reflective mode. The quote should be short and relevant.

Aromatherapy. Aromas play to the sense of smell. It can be appealing to have incense burning during the Circle time. Some aboriginal circles use the burning of sage at the start of a Circle to clear the air and to mark the beginning of a council session.

Food or drink. A common ritual that is often overlooked is food or drink. Sharing a snack or beverage brings us closer. One easy way to do this is to designate a food bearer for each meeting. This way a different person would be responsible for bringing the food each time.

Personal items. Some Circles start each meeting by placing a personal object in the center of the Circle. This is symbolic of bringing themselves into the Circle. To enhance this ritual, the members can explain the significance of the object. These stories can be very powerful and can provide a great ice-breaker for the group.

This One Circle Process, when used in conjunction with the Circle Principles and Circle Practices brings together all the ingredients necessary to create a powerful Circle, a meaningful conversation and a resilient group. The next two chapters provide scripts and instructions to help you conduct the first six critical Circle meetings.

Chapter 6
....
The First Three Meetings

We are all longing to go home to some place we have never been – a place, half-remembered and half-envisioned, we can only catch glimpses of from time to time. Community. Somewhere, there are people to whom we can speak with passion without having the words catch in our throats. Somewhere a circle of hands will open to receive us, eyes will light up as we enter, voices will celebrate us whenever we come into our own power.... Someplace where we can be free.

—Starhawk, *Dreaming the Dark*

The first few meetings are critical to the success of the Circle. During these meetings not only do the individuals begin to build relationships, but they agree to the fundamental principles that form the foundation for all their future Circle meetings. This chapter provides detailed instructions and scripts for the first three meetings. The next chapter concludes with a sample agenda that can be used at any Circle meeting.

Although much of the first few meetings will be on getting acquainted and sorting out logistics, the core of the discussions will be about the Circle Principles, Practices and Process and creating a Circle Purpose Statement. After that the members will begin to share their goals and aspirations. It is worthwhile not to rush through the first few meetings. These meetings form the basis for the rest.

In terms of overall objectives, by the end of the first three meetings the group should understand why they are meeting in a Circle, how they will act in the Circle and what their responsibilities will be. By the third meeting, members should all do the following:

- agree with the Circle Principles
- agree to apply the Circle Practices
- understand the Circle Process
- draft a Circle Purpose Statement
- commit to the Circle

If you decide to keep a Circle journal, you can list these as the anticipated outcomes of the first three meetings.

Meeting 1. Introductions, Circle basics, expectations and logistics

There's a lot to cover in the initial meeting of the Circle, so it helps to prepare an agenda and some written objectives beforehand.

Introductions

Because people often come to the first meeting a bit nervous and excited, it is useful to begin with personal introductions and an overview of what the first meeting is about. Once everyone is seated in the circle, the Circle Guide should use a script like the following:

> **Script:** *Welcome and thanks for coming. Over the next hour and a half we will meet each other and I will provide you with information about the Circle Process. This meeting will not be an actual Circle meeting, but rather an introduction to each other and to the Circle Process. By the end of the meeting you should know what a Circle is, what happens in a Circle and what is expected of you. We will hold our first formal Circle at our next meeting. Before we begin it might be useful to go around the circle and have everyone introduce themselves and say a bit about how they heard about Circles. I will start. Are there any questions?*

Circle basics

Once everyone has introduced themselves, the guide provides a short presentation on Circles. This includes information on where Circles come from and why they are unique. Here is the list of items to cover:

- What is a Circle?
- The benefits of Circles
- What Circles are not

- The origins of Circles

- Why Circles work

You will notice that this list follows the contents of chapter 1, so when preparing for the first meeting, the guide will want to review that chapter. Here is a script to introduce this part. You can present the talking piece at the same time.

> **Script:** *For the next half hour or so, I will provide you with an overview of the Circle Process. Feel free to ask questions as we go along. I will leave time for questions at the end as well. We will then sort out some of the logistics for future meetings.*
>
> *Although I am acting as the Circle Guide today and for the next few meetings, at our next meeting we will discuss how we want this role to be filled. Usually the Circle Guide role rotates among the members.*
>
> *As you can see I have brought a talking piece. I use it as a tool to promote conversation. It is passed from person to person as they speak. Later we can decide whether we want a talking piece and what it should be. Any questions? Now let me tell you a bit about the Circle Principles, Practices and Process.*

The guide can then provide a summary of the three fundamental parts of the Circle: the Circle Principles, Practices and Process. It is useful to provide a handout like the one on the next page. You will not discuss these in much detail at the first meeting, but the list provides a good overview.

One Circle Principles, Practices and Process

One Circle Principles

- Equality
- Confidentiality
- Commitment
- Shared ownership
- Shared leadership

One Circle Practices

- Intention
- Speaking
- Listening
- Guiding

The One Circle Process

- Preparing for the Circle
- The Opening
- The Check-In
- Topic Selection
- The Conversation
- The Check-Out
- The Closing

Expectations

After the presentation it is useful to have a brief conversation about the expectations that each person has of the Circle. This begins the process of identifying the purpose of your particular Circle. This conversation will be continued at the next meeting. Here is a script you might want to use:

> **Script:** *As you know, at the next few meetings we will be discussing the Circle Principles, Practices and Process in more detail. One of the principles is shared ownership, which means we all share in the functioning of the Circle. To support this principle, most Circles adopt a Circle Purpose Statement, which describes the shared purpose of the group. We can begin that process of drafting a Circle Purpose Statement today by going around the circle and sharing our own individual reasons for joining this Circle. At the third meeting we will discuss our purpose statement in more detail and perhaps come to some agreement on it. Sam, do you want to start? Perhaps we can pass the talking piece around.*

Logistics

The last item to be discussed at the first meeting is logistics. Rather than going around the circle, it is best if the group simply talks about what works best for them. The questions to address are as follows:

- Where will you meet?
- How long will you meet?
- When will you meet?

- Whom will you invite?
- Who will be the temporary Circle Guide?

Closing

At all future Circle meetings there will be a formal Check-Out and Closing. For the first meeting it is sufficient to simply pass the talking piece around and ask the members to identify one thing they learned and to ask any questions. Here is a sample script:

> **Script:** *I will now bring this meeting to a close. As you know, this meeting was not an actual Circle meeting, but rather an introduction to each other and an introduction to the Circle Principles, Practices and Process. You should now have an idea about what a Circle is, what happens in a Circle and what is expected of you. We will hold our first formal Circle at our next meeting. Before closing, perhaps we can simply pass the talking piece around and describe one thing that each of us learned and ask any questions.*

Ideally there should be some relaxed social time or sharing of refreshments after the meeting.

Meeting 2. The Circle Process, Principles and Practices

The second meeting is the first formal Circle meeting. This means that the Circle Process is used and the guide is responsible for leading the group through the process. It is important to keep in mind that the Circle Process has several components that play a unique role in creating a safe and welcoming place. Each step is important and should not be rushed through or skipped.

The second meeting is dedicated to discussing the Circle Process, Principles and Practices. If there is time, the group can begin to create their Circle Purpose Statement.

Before the meeting the guide will need to prepare for the Circle. This means selecting a talking piece, purchasing a journal, preparing an agenda and preparing the space. The guide may also want to bring a poem or a quotation for the Opening and the Closing and some questions for the Check-In and the Check-Out. The agenda for the second meeting will be as follows:

- The Opening

- The Check-In

- Topic Selection: Preselected

- The Conversation: The Circle Process, Principles and Practices

- The Check-Out

- The Closing

Here are sample scripts for each of these parts:

The Opening

Script: *Hello and welcome back. At our last meeting I provided an overview of the Circle Principles, Practices and Process. We then had a brief conversa-*

tion about our reasons for joining this Circle and got to know each other a bit better. This meeting will be our first Circle meeting. This means I will follow the Circle Process in conducting our conversations. [Pause] Thank you all for coming. I will open the Circle with a short quotation. I will then invite you each to check in with a few words about how you feel and what you expect in today's Circle. [Read quotation]

The Check-In

Script: *Now that I have formally opened the Circle, we will do a check-in. I will pass around the talking piece. You will each have about two minutes to say how you are feeling and what you hope to achieve in this particular Circle. [Pass around the talking piece]*

Topic Selection

Script: *In a regular Circle meeting, at this point we would select a topic for discussion. Because this is our second meeting, we will be discussing the Circle Process, Principles and Practices that will form the foundation for all our future meetings. I have decided to use the talking piece method of conversation, which means that I introduce the topic and then pass the piece around to each of you for your comments. You may pass the piece on without speaking if you wish.*

The Conversation

Script: *As you recall, at our last meeting I briefly described the Circle Process, Principles and Practices. I provided a one-page summary. At this meeting we will discuss each of these with the goal of better understanding what they mean. At the end of the meeting, we should be able to agree to the Circle Principles and Circle Practices and better understand the Circle Process.*

Discussing the Circle Process

Script: *As you can see, I am following the Circle Process, which consists of the following seven parts:*

1. *Preparing for the Circle*

2. *The Opening*

3. *The Check-In*

4. *Topic Selection*

5. *The Conversation*

6. *The Check-Out*

7. *The Closing*

I prepared for the Circle by selecting a talking piece, purchasing a journal, preparing an agenda and preparing the space. I also brought a quotation for the Opening and the Closing, and I prepared a question for the Check-In and for the Check-Out. I just opened the Circle, guided you through the Check-In and introduced today's topic.

I will now pass around the talking piece to see if there are any questions or comments about the Circle Process so far. [Pass around the talking piece]

Discussing the Circle Principles

It is useful to discuss the Circle Principles as a whole group, since they form the foundation of the whole Circle Process. They are essentially the rules that must be followed to make the Circle successful. Recall they are equality, confidentiality, commitment, shared ownership and shared leadership.

Some Circles simply adopt the Circle Principles and move on. Others prefer to design their own principles using the Circle Principles as a base for discussion. Although either approach is fine, a conversation about principles is very useful. This is because a conversation about principles is really a conversation about values. It is about each member's philosophies on how they will show up and participate in the Circle. The conversation allows each person to talk about what these principles mean to them. Since there are rarely two people who feel exactly the same about the Circle Principles, speaking about them gives them some depth and practical application.

Although many might see these Circle Principles as fairly obvious or motherhood statements, it is rare to find a group that has adopted these principles verbatim. This demonstrates how Circles are unique and so effective at promoting candid conversations.

An easy way to begin a discussion about principles is to have the guide review the Circle Principles, then go around the Circle and have the members describe what the principles mean to them. Individuals may share stories about other group experiences or speak about the principles that are most relevant to them. Here is a sample script:

> **Script:** *As you know, there are five Circle Principles that form the foundation of the Circle Process. The effectiveness of our Circle depends on the extent to which we follow these principles. I think it is useful to have a discussion about the principles to help us understand what they mean and to help us bring them to life through personal experiences. I would like to pass around the talking piece and have each of us talk briefly about what the principles mean to us. I invite you to share stories about your experiences. Before we begin, I will review each of them and what they mean to me.*

- ○ *Equality...*
- ○ *Confidentiality...*
- ○ *Commitment...*
- ○ *Shared ownership...*
- ○ *Shared leadership...*

Regardless of the type of conversation, by the end of the discussion, the group should understand what the Circle Principles mean and agree to adhere to these principles when they are in the Circle.

Discussing the Circle Practices

It is useful to briefly discuss the Circle Practices, because they are the skills that each of the members agrees to apply in the Circle. Some Circles simply review the description of the Practices provided in chapter 4. Others prefer a more lengthy conversation. Here is a sample script for the discussion of Practices:

> **Script:** *As you know, there are four Circle Practices that form the second aspect of the Circle Process. The effectiveness of the Circle will increase as members become more skilled at these practices. They reflect the principles in action. I think it is useful to have a discussion about the practices to help us understand what they are and how they could be applied in the Circle. We may also want to discuss how we can help develop these practices personally and while in the Circle. I will review the four practices and my understanding of what they mean, then pass around the talking piece to hear your comments and experiences. Here is my understanding of the Circle Practices:*
>
> ○ *Intention means...*
>
> ○ *Speaking means...*
>
> ○ *Listening means...*
>
> ○ *Guiding means...*

The guide will want to provide a formal conclusion to the conversation before moving to the Check-Out. To do this, the guide can either pass around the talking piece one last time and seek concluding comments from each of the members or can provide a summary or concluding comments. Here is sample script:

> **Script:** *We have covered a lot of ground today. I think it is fair to say we each have a better understanding about the Circle Process, Principles and Practices. As mentioned at the beginning of the*

discussion, the goal of this meeting was to have us
each agree to the principles and practices and to have
a better understanding of the process. I think we are
there, but I would like your final comments before
moving to the Check-Out. Who would like to start?

The Check-Out

After the Conversation there is a brief Check-Out. The members pass the talking piece around the Circle and briefly say
how they are feeling and one thing they learned. Here is a
sample script:

> **Script:** *It is now time to conclude our meeting. We
> do this by passing around the talking piece and
> checking out. Then I close the Circle. This has been a
> very productive Circle meeting. I get the sense that we
> have accomplished a lot. For the Check-Out I would
> like to pass around the talking piece one last time to
> find out how people feel and what they have learned.
> Please also feel free to mention any outstanding
> issues and any ideas about ways to improve the Circle
> process. If we do not have time to discuss these issues
> today I will bring them back at the beginning of the
> next meeting. Kelly, do you want to start?*

During the Check-Out, the guide will write down anything
that needs to be brought forward at the next meeting.

The Closing

After the Check-Out there is a formal Closing. Here is a
sample script:

Script: *I am calling this Circle to a close. Thank you for engaging in this conversation. I would like to close with the following quotation. [Read quotation] Thank you to [name each member] for participating today. I welcome you all to join me for refreshments.*

Meeting 3. The Circle Purpose Statement and the Circle Guide

The third meeting is the second formal Circle meeting. This means that the guide will again lead the group through the Circle Process. The third meeting is dedicated to discussing the Circle Purpose Statement and the role of the Circle Guide.

As with all Circle meetings, the guide will need to prepare for the Circle by preparing an agenda, preparing the space and by bringing a talking piece, a journal, quotations and questions. The agenda for the second meeting is as follows:

- The Opening

- The Check-In

- Topic Selection: Preselected

- The Conversation: The Circle Purpose Statement and the Circle Guide

- The Check-Out

- The Closing

Here are sample scripts for each of these parts:

The Opening

Script: *Hello and welcome to our third meeting. At our last meeting we discussed and agreed to the Circle Principles, Practices and Process. These form the foundation of all of our future meetings. They can be reviewed or revised as we evolve. This meeting will be our second Circle meeting. This means I will again follow the Circle Process in conducting our conversations. [Pause] Thank you all for coming. I will open the Circle with a short quotation. I will then invite you each to check in with a few words about how you feel and what you expect in today's Circle. [Read quotation]*

The Check-In

Script: *Now that I have formally opened the Circle, we will do a check-in. I will pass around the talking piece. You will each have about two minutes to say how you are feeling and what you hope to achieve in this particular Circle. [Pass around the talking piece]*

Topic Selection

Script: *In a regular Circle meeting, at this point we would select a topic for discussion. Because this is our third meeting, will be discussing our Circle Purpose Statement and the role of the Circle Guide. I have decided to use the talking piece method of conversation, which means that I introduce the topic and then pass around the talking piece for each of your com-*

ments. You may pass the piece on without speaking if you wish.

The Conversation

During the Conversation stage, the group will discuss both the Circle Purpose Statement and the role of the Circle Guide.

Discussing the Circle Purpose Statement

Script: *As you know, one of the Circle Principles is shared ownership, which means we each share in the functioning of the Circle. To support this principle, most Circles adopt a Circle Purpose Statement, which describes the shared purpose of the group. You may recall our first meeting, when we went around the Circle and shared our own individual reasons for joining this Circle. This began the process of figuring out how the Circle can best serve each of us. Perhaps we can do this again today and add a bit more detail. Who wants to take the talking piece and talk about why they want to be part of a Circle?*

Once the members have shared their personal reasons for joining, there should be a brief discussion about the group purpose. Since this conversation can be time-consuming, it is best initially to adopt a general statement that can be revised later. After you have spent some time together, you will have a better idea about what brings you all together and how you can help each other. Here are some samples of general Circle Purpose Statements. You may want to adopt all or parts of these for your first draft.

Entrepreneur Circle. Our Circle is primarily for the purpose of helping each other build our businesses. We want to learn about how to attract great clients and run our businesses as effectively and efficiently as possible.

Executive Circle. Our Circle is primarily for the purpose of helping each other become better leaders and business owners. We want to be more effective in business, in life and in our communities.

Corporate mentoring Circle. Our Circle is primarily to bring together senior and junior people for purposes of sharing knowledge and skills. This will help the organization plan for succession and will help each individual develop professionally, learn practical skills and gain leadership traits.

Professional women's Circle. Our Circle is primarily to provide support and advice in our personal and professional pursuits. We will help each other be successful (however we each define this) and find balance between home and work.

Parenting Circle. Our Circle is primarily to share parenting experiences (good and bad) and learn about how to be a great parent. The topics that interest us most are dealing with teenagers, discipline and dealing with aging parents.

Career change Circle. Our Circle is primarily to help each other get the most out of our working lives and find careers that are best suited to our skills and interests. We are most interested in job search skills, resumé building and networking.

Discussing the role of the Circle Guide

One of the unique features of the Circle Process is the role of the Circle Guide. The guide leads the Circle Process and is responsible for making sure that the Circle runs smoothly from beginning to end. Functions of a Circle Guide include arranging the Circle meeting, leading the group through the Circle steps, keeping track of time and ensuring that topics are fully discussed.

At the third meeting the group should discuss how they wish to deal with the role of the guide. They need to decide who will be the guide at each meeting (internal or external) and how the role will rotate or change between members. Here is a sample script:

> **Script:** *As you know, each Circle must have a Circle Guide. This role involves arranging the meetings and guiding the Circle Process at the meetings. I have played this role for these first few meetings. We now need to discuss how we want this role to be played in the future. We can choose an internal guide or an external guide. We must decide how long that person will stay in the role of guide and when the role will be taken by someone else. It is recommended that the role of Circle Guide be rotated among all the members – usually for a few months at a time. This reflects the principles of equality, shared leadership and shared ownership. I will pass around the talking piece, and we can share our thoughts on how to handle the role of Circle Guide.*

The Check-Out

> **Script:** *It is now time to end our meeting. This has been a very productive Circle meeting. I get the sense that we have really begun to bond and are more open in our conversations. For the Check-Out I have two questions: How do you feel? and What have you learned? I would also like your feedback on the Circle Process and any outstanding items. Diane, do you want to start?*

The Closing

> **Script:** *I am calling this Circle to a close. Thank you for providing such a great conversation. I would like to close with the following quotation:*
>
> *[Read quotation] Thank you all for participating today. I welcome you all to join me for refreshments.*

During these first three meetings, members of the Circle gain the necessary understanding about the One Circle Process that will guide them for the remainder of their time together. Ideally the One Circle Principles, Practices and Process will be reviewed periodically. As they are applied in practice they will become more meaningful and their importance will be recognized. These fundamentals must always be revisited when problems arise, as described in chapter 8. The fourth, fifth and sixth meetings are equally important, as discussed in the next chapter.

Chapter 7
....

The Next Three Meetings

The circle is neither a solution to our problems nor a magic wand that makes all our problems instantly disappear. It is more like a missing piece of social technology, which enables us to tap into a latent capacity for wisdom, collective support, and insight.

—Carolyn Boyes-Watson

The next three meetings are designed to help members get to know each other better. The content of these meetings is based on my book *Mission Possible: Creating a Mission for Work and Life.* If you wish to learn more about how to do the exercises in these three meetings, you should refer to this book.

This chapter provides detailed instructions and scripts for the fourth, fifth and sixth meetings. At the end is a sample agenda that can be used at any Circle meeting. These three meetings build a foundation of understanding about each of the members of the Circle. This understanding enables each of the members to contribute to discussions to assist each of the other members be their best, achieve their goals and overcome any obstacles. By the end of the sixth meeting, the group will have a good understanding of each member's vision, mission and goals. These will form the foundation of the group's conversations over the succeeding months.

Meeting 4. Creating a vision statement

The fourth meeting is the first chance for the group to share information about themselves with the group. This meeting is dedicated to having each person create their own personal or professional vision statement.

Creating this vision is a foundation for future learning and growing in the Circle. The extent to which the Circle can assist each member depends to a large degree on how well the group knows each person and their aspirations. Since the Circle is designed to help each member achieve success, one of the first steps is defining what success means to each person. This can be done most simply by having each person create a vision statement.

The agenda for the fourth meeting, similar to the other meetings, is as follows:

- The Opening

- The Check-In

- Topic Selection: Preselected

- The Conversation: Creating a vision statement

- The Check-Out
- The Closing

Here are some scripts for this meeting:

The Opening

Script: *Hello and welcome to our fourth meeting. As you know, our first three meetings were dedicated to learning about the Circle Principles, Practices and Process; learning about the role of the Circle Guide; and creating our own Circle Purpose Statement. The next three meetings are dedicated to getting to know each other better. To do this we will be defining our own vision, identifying our own uniqueness and developing our personal mission statements. By working on these in the Circle we learn more about each other and create a foundation of understanding for the remaining life of this Circle.*

I will again follow the Circle Process in conducting our conversations. [Pause] Thank you all for coming. I will open the Circle with a short quotation. I will then invite you each to check in with a few words about how you feel and what you expect in today's Circle. [Read quotation]

The Check-In

Script: *Now that I have formally opened the Circle, we will do a check-in. I will pass around the talking piece. You will each have about two minutes to say how you are feeling and what you hope to achieve in this particular Circle. [Pass around the talking piece]*

141

Topic Selection

Script: *In a regular Circle meeting, at this point we would select a topic for discussion. Because this is our fourth meeting, will be creating and discussing our vision statements. I will use the talking piece method of conversation, which means that I will introduce the topic and then pass around the talking piece to hear each of your comments.*

The Conversation

During this part of the meeting each person will need a blank piece of paper or a personal journal. The Circle Guide will explain what a vision statement is and then ask questions that will help the members create their own vision statement. Individuals may then wish to share their vision in the Circle.

Script: *Please take out a piece of paper or your journal. I will tell you a bit about vision statements, then will ask you some questions to help you identify your own vision. Then, if you wish, you can share your vision with the group.*

A vision statement describes the end result of what you want to have achieved in your life. It is a picture of what your life will look like after you have lived it. It is your ideal life. It is your personal definition of success. Its main purpose is to provide an ultimate goal so you will know where you want to end up and when you have arrived. Each person's vision will be different and entirely unique.

Creating a vision involves creating a picture of where you will be when you are successful. The easiest way to do this is to try to imagine what success looks like.

I will pass the talking stick around the Circle. I would like each person to imagine themselves twenty years from now and describe this in detail. Before I do that, I will read a few questions that will help you in creating this vision. After I ask the questions, I will leave a few minutes for people to write down their thoughts.

1. *Where are you living?*
   - *Your city?*
   - *Your view?*
   - *Your community or neighborhood?*
   - *Are you inside or outside?*
   - *Are you near nature?*

2. *What is your work or business?*
   - *What are you doing?*
   - *Your work setting or industry?*
   - *Your work and functions?*
   - *Your volunteer activities?*
   - *What are you wearing?*

3. *Who are you with?*
   - *Your clients?*
   - *Your family?*
   - *Your friends?*

○   *Your clubs or communities?*

○   *Your religious or spiritual group?*

4.   *What are you good at?*

○   *Your skills, abilities, knowledge?*

○   *Your personal characteristics or qualities?*

○   *Your demeanor?*

○   *Your approach?*

5.   *What are your leisure activities?*

○   *Your travels?*

○   *Your hobbies or crafts?*

○   *Your social life?*

○   *Your home?*

○   *Your garden?*

6.   *What is your lifestyle?*

○   *Your health?*

○   *Your fitness?*

○   *Your stress level?*

○   *Your weight?*

○   *Are you smoking?*

7.   *What do you possess?*

○   *Your home?*

○   *Your car?*

○   *Your wardrobe?*

○   *Your toys?*

○   *Retirement savings?*

After going around the Circle, the guide will ask each person to write down their own vision statement. Here is a format that is fairly easy to use.

I AM A SUCCESS ...

I am _____ [doing]

I am _____ [living]

I am _____ [spending time with], etc.

After each member writes down their own vision statement, they can share it with the group if they wish and pass around the talking piece again.

The Check-Out

Script: *It is now time to end our meeting. This has been a very interesting Circle meeting. We have really learned a lot about each other and our aspirations. For the Check-Out I have two questions: How do you feel? and What have you learned? I would also like your feedback on the Circle Process and any outstanding items. Jane, do you want to start?*

The Closing

Script: *I am calling this Circle to a close. Thank you for providing such a wonderful conversation. I would like to close with the following quotation. [Read quotation] Thank you all for participating today. I welcome you all to join me for refreshments.*

Meeting 5. Identifying your uniqueness

The fifth Circle meeting is dedicated to identifying the uniqueness of each member. This means defining each person's unique knowledge, skills, interests and talents.

In order for the group to be able to help each person, members need to know who each person is and what makes them unique. With this information, members will be better able to advise others. As well, by understanding their own particular skills and knowledge, each of the members will be better able to direct their actions in a way that is consistent with their uniqueness.

The agenda for the fifth meeting is as follows:

- The Opening

- The Check-In

- Topic Selection: Preselected

- The Conversation: Identifying your uniqueness

- The Check-Out

- The Closing

Here are some sample scripts for this meeting:

The Opening

Script: *Hello and welcome to our fifth meeting. At our last meeting we created our own personal vision statements. At this meeting we will be identifying our own uniqueness. The better we understand each* *other's uniqueness, the better able we will be to help each other. Also, by articulating our own uniqueness we will be better able to align this uniqueness with what we do. I will again follow the Circle Process in conducting our conversations. [Pause] Thank you all for coming. I will open the Circle with a short quotation. I will then invite you each to check in with a few words about how you feel and what you expect in today's Circle. [Read quotation]*

The Check-In

Script: *Now that I have formally opened the Circle, we will do a check-in. I will pass around the talking piece. You will each have a few minutes to say how you are feeling and what you hope to achieve in this particular Circle. [Pass around the talking piece]*

Topic Selection

Script: *In a regular Circle meeting, at this point we would select a topic for discussion. Because this is our fifth meeting, we will be identifying our uniqueness. I will use the talking piece method of conversation, which means that I will introduce the topic and then pass the piece around the talking piece for each of your comments.*

The Conversation

Each person will need a blank piece of paper or a personal journal. The Circle Guide will explain what is meant by uniqueness and introduce a technique for identifying uniqueness. Each member will define their uniqueness, then have an opportunity to share it with the group

> **Script:** *An easy way to begin thinking about uniqueness is by describing yourself in terms of a metaphor. A metaphor is a picture description of something not human. I will pass around the talking stick and ask each of you to describe yourself in terms of a metaphor. Samples of metaphors include a tree, a car, an elevator, a shoe, a roller coaster, a river, a hot air balloon, a guitar, a hang glider, skis, a motor boat and a seed. Once you have chosen your metaphor, I will pass around the talking piece again and ask you to describe your metaphor in more detail. At that time I will ask a few questions to stimulate your thinking. I will give you all a few minutes to think about your metaphor before beginning. [Pass around the talking piece]*
>
> *Now that we know your metaphor, I would like you to describe it in more detail. I will read a few questions to stimulate your thinking, then I will pass around the talking piece again. Here are the questions:*
>
> ○ *What does it look like?*
>
> ○ *What shape is it?*
>
> ○ *How does it move or function?*
>
> ○ *Is it big or small?*
>
> ○ *What is the color?*

○ *Where has it been?*

○ *Is it worn out?*

○ *What is it doing?*

○ *What is the environment around it?*

○ *Is it tired?*

○ *Is it in need of repair?*

○ *It is solid and sturdy?*

○ *Is it capable of growth and change?*

After reading these questions, the guide should allow time for the members to write down their thoughts on their metaphor. The aim is to help each member identify their unique knowledge, skills, abilities, interests and talents. After members have had enough time, the talking piece is passed around again. Here is a script:

> **Script:** *This exercise was designed to help you identify your unique knowledge, skills, abilities, interests and talents. I will pass around the talking piece once more so that each of you has an opportunity to share what you learned about your uniqueness. [Pass around the talking piece]*

The Check-Out

> **Script:** *It is now time to end our meeting. This has been an informative Circle meeting. We have really learned a lot about each other's uniqueness. For the Check-Out I have two questions: How do you feel? and What have you learned? I would also like your*

feedback on the Circle Process and any outstanding items. Bob, do you want to start?

The Closing

Script: *I am calling this Circle to a close. Thank you for providing such an enjoyable conversation. I would like to close with the following quotation. [Read quotation] Thank you all for participating today. I welcome you all to join me for refreshments.*

Meeting 6. Developing a mission statement and setting goals

The sixth meeting is dedicated to helping each member define their own personal mission statement and set some goals. A mission statement is a statement of purpose and direction. It describes what you want to achieve in life and work and provides both a beacon and a measure of success personally and professionally. Your mission statement flows directly from your vision and your uniqueness. It describes how each person will reach their vision in a way that is consistent with who they are.

The agenda for the sixth meeting is as follows:

- The Opening
- The Check-In
- Topic Selection: Preselected
- The Conversation: Creating a personal mission statement and setting goals

- The Check-Out

- The Closing

Here are some sample scripts for this meeting:

The Opening

Script: *Hello and welcome to our sixth meeting. As you know, this will be the last of our foundation-setting meetings. In the first three meetings we learned about the Circle Process; in the last two meetings we learned about our vision and our uniqueness. Today the discussion will focus on our personal mission statements. As we learn more about each other, we create a strong foundation for all of our future Circles.*

I will again follow the Circle Process in conducting our conversations. [Pause] Thank you all for coming. I will open the Circle with a short quotation. I will then invite you each to check in with a few words about how you feel and what you expect in today's Circle. [Read quotation]

The Check-In

Script: *Now that I have formally opened the Circle, we will do a check-in. I will pass around the talking piece. You will each have about two minutes to say how you are feeling and what you hope to achieve in this particular Circle. [Pass around the talking piece]*

Topic Selection

> **Script:** *Because this is our fifth meeting, will be developing and discussing our personal and professional mission statements. I will use the talking piece method of conversation, which means that I will introduce the topic, then pass around the talking piece for each of your comments.*

The Conversation

Each person will need a blank piece of paper or a personal journal. The Circle Guide will explain what a mission statement is and then ask questions that will help the members create their own mission statement. Individuals may then wish to share their mission statement in the Circle.

> **Script:** *Before beginning this part of the meeting, recall your vision and uniqueness from the last two meetings. If you wrote them down, pull them out.*
>
> *A mission statement is a statement of purpose and direction. It is a reason for being. It describes what you want to achieve in life and work and provides both a beacon and a measure of success personally and professionally. Your mission statement flows directly from your vision and uniqueness. It describes how you will reach your vision in a way that is consistent with who you are. It reflects the uniqueness of you and your work.*
>
> *Each mission statement contains three fundamental pieces: an Action, an Audience or focus, and an*

Accomplishment or outcome. The Action represents what you would like to do. It is a verb or action word. The Audience represents the people you would like to focus on, and the Accomplishment is the result or outcome. It is the change you want to bring about to your audience. For example, one mission is to inspire (Action) leaders (Audience) to bring about positive change (Accomplishment).

When creating your mission, the question you want to ask yourself is: What Action will I take, for what people or Audience, and for what results or Accomplishment? The following is the form of a mission statement:

My mission is to ...

Action: _____

Audience: _____

Accomplishment: _____

I will give you all a few minutes to reflect on your own mission, then I will pass around the talking piece so you can share your mission statement if you wish. After that we can engage in an open question-and-answer period to help each other refine our mission statements.

The Check-Out

Script: *It is now time to end our meeting. This has been a very informative Circle meeting. We have* *really learned a lot about each other's missions. For the Check-Out I have two questions: How do you feel? and What have you learned? I would also like your feedback on the Circle Process and any outstanding items. Emily, do you want to start?*

The Closing

Script: *I am calling this Circle to a close. Thank you for providing such a great conversation. I would like to close with the following quotation. [Read quotation] Thank you all for participating today. I welcome you all to join me for refreshments.*

The remaining meetings

By the end of the sixth meeting, the group should have a solid foundation and be able to begin having conversations that are relevant and meaningful to them at each meeting.

All of the remaining Circle meetings will follow a similar pattern. However, unlike the first six meetings, the topic of conversation will not be predetermined. Like the first few meetings, the Circle will have a designated Circle Guide who will prepare for the meeting and lead the group through the Circle Process.

On the following page is a Circle meeting agenda that can be used at each of the remaining meetings. The next chapter explains how to maintain and evaluate your Circle and specifically how to deal with difficult situations.

Sample Circle meeting agenda

Preparation

- Prepare an agenda.
- Select a talking piece.
- Bring a journal.
- Bring a script, quotations and questions.
- Prepare the space.

Opening (5 minutes)

- Welcome everyone.
- Mention any news or celebrations.
- Discuss any outstanding items.

The Check-In (3–5 minutes each person)

- Pass the talking piece around the Circle.
- Ask: How do you feel? and What are your hopes for this Circle?

Topic Selection (5 minutes)

- Do you have a preselected topic? If so, go to the Conversation.
- Do you want to select a topic now? If so, allow some reflection time, then pass around the talking piece.
- Ask either: What would you like to discuss? or ask a reflective question.
- Select the topic(s) for discussion.

The Conversation (1–2 hours)

- Select a mode of conversation.
  - ○ talking piece method
  - ○ brainstorming method
  - ○ decision-making method
- Discuss topic(s).
- Conclude (summarize or pass the talking piece).

The Check-Out (2 minutes each person)

- Pass the talking piece around the circle.
- Ask: How do you feel? and Can you name one thing you learned in this Circle?
- Ask: Any questions or ideas for improving the process?

The Closing (3 minutes)

- Mention any carryover items.
- Thank you and good-bye.

Chapter 8

....

Maintain and Evaluate Your Circle

*Many of us hunger for a serious commitment. . . .
What counts overall is the quality of exchange that
occurs when you do get together. A group that
meets monthly, or even quarterly and engages at
deep levels of truth-telling can feel more
committed than a group that meets weekly but is
stuck in "terminal niceness" and manages only a
superficial dialogue.*

—Charles A. Garfield et al., *Wisdom Circles*

Even the best-run Circle will run into problems periodically. The problems can be sudden or slow to emerge.
They can be about simple things such as members being late
for meetings to complex things such as continual silence or

interruptions. Three other situations that every Circle will face are the addition of a member, the departure of a member and the end of a Circle. All problems should be dealt with as quickly as possible and with care.

This chapter explains how to deal with difficult situations and how to troubleshoot typical problems that arise in Circles. It explains how to deal with new members and departing members and ends with a technique for evaluating your Circle.

Problems are natural

It is important to keep in mind that problems and disputes are natural occurrences in any group and should be dealt with as such. The group should look at them as something that will definitely occur and as an opportunity to reaffirm the understandings and workings of the Circle.

Circles are much like living organisms that evolve depending on the mix of people and the context, some more quickly than others. The health of a Circle can be measured in large part by how well it deals with differences. Indeed, the growth of a Circle depends on how well it resolves conflict. For example, if a member raises an issue and then feels attacked, it may take months for that Circle to feel safe again. Disputes that are dealt with respectfully will lead to more authentic conversations, as reflected here:

> Council that avoids openly dealing with its unhealthy dynamics loses power to communicate in a trusting way and so misses the opportunity for greater intimacy. Eventually the councils become superficial and flounder.[1]

Sometimes problems arise as a result of growth. The growth and evolution of each Circle should be encouraged, even when it might seem difficult. If individuals feel the Circle is not meeting their goals, this must be addressed. If the topics are not relevant, this must be addressed. If someone is interrupting repeatedly, this must be addressed. If a member is preventing the development of the Circle, this too must be addressed.

If a Circle is not open or tends to be too stiff or inflexible, members will eventually feel it does not fit or accommodate their needs. As members' needs change, so must the Circle.

As you will see below, the way to resolve differences is through conversation. But more important is the intent that each person brings to the conversation. Armed with the intent to make the Circle the best it can be, most members will find a way to say what they need to say in a candid yet compassionate way. Remember, it's not *what* you say, but *how* you say it that makes the difference. If each member starts with the shared intention to keep the Circle relevant and strong, each of the skills and techniques described here can be applied successfully.

Dealing with difficult situations

If a Circle is not functioning properly, each person will feel it to some extent or other. Members will slowly stop sharing, and open communication will dwindle. A sense of awkwardness is one of the first signs that something is wrong. At this point each member should be thinking about doing something. It does not matter if others think something is wrong or not, but likely at least one other person in the Circle feels the awkwardness too.

Here are the main ways to deal with difficult situations:

- Face your fear of conflict.
- Lay a foundation of responsibility.
- Clarify expectations to prevent disputes.
- Use the three Fs to resolve conflict.

Face your fear of conflict

There will be many times in a Circle when communication will be difficult. A member might be speaking too much, or a topic might be too controversial or personal. Rather than talk about it, however, many of us flee from conflict. We engage in a conflict avoidance thinking loop that prevents a necessary conversation from occurring. In our minds we think either that the problem is so serious that it cannot be resolved or we think that the person cannot or will not change. This thinking prevents us from trying to resolve the issue at all. When we do this we do not engage in a conversation. In a Circle, fear of confrontation will cause members to either stop speaking or silently contemplate leaving.

These thoughts must be challenged and replaced with more realistic thoughts. If you catch yourself thinking these things, try to tell yourself that on this occasion you might be wrong. This problem may be solvable and this person may be open to change. Unless you do this, all attempts at resolution will fail before you even begin.

By facing your initial fear of conflict, taking responsibility and using the tools described here, you will be able to deal with most differences as they arise. Remember, the solution to conflict is conversation, but each member of the Circle must have the courage to begin the conversation.

Lay a foundation of responsibility

Unlike other groups, the responsibility of maintaining the Circle rests with each and every one of its members. Each member commits to the other members, to the Circle as a whole and to the Circle Process, and therefore members are personally responsible for themselves and for alerting others about their needs or concerns. The Circle Guide can help resolve disputes but can only do so much to keep the group growing in a constructive way and moving in a healthy direction.

Whenever there is a conflict, each member should start by looking at things from three perspectives: an individual perspective, the perspective of other members, and the Circle's perspective. In other words, a person who is sensing conflict should ask three questions:

- How is this impacting me?

- How is this impacting others?

- How is this impacting the Circle?

Imagine the following internal conversation that you might have while sitting in the Circle:

Real life. Barb has been talking nonstop for fifteen minutes. Since her husband left her, it seems as if the entire focus of our Circle has been on her

161

problems. I like and respect Barb and do not mind listening, but I am tired. I feel frustrated that I am not able to help her. I am also frustrated because we are not talking about the things that are of concern to others. Because Barb is so sensitive and vulnerable at this time, it would seem selfish of me to ask her to reduce her speaking time. The only thing I can do is sit and wait or quit.

In this thought pattern, the member is assuming that the problem cannot be resolved and that Barb cannot change. This thinking loop caused him to give up trying and remain silent. If you ask yourself the three questions posed above, here is what you might discover:

Personal impact: I am wasting valuable time. I am feeling frustrated. I am afraid to say anything for fear of looking insensitive. I feel angry that I don't have the courage to speak up. I know I am responsible for my own needs, but I feel stuck. I am not sure this Circle can meet my needs. Surely others must feel as I do.

Member impact: I can see that others are zoning out. Last week Barb said she felt bad for taking up all the Circle time. Others might be relieved if I speak up. Barb won't likely be hurt if I speak authentically but gently. I know Barb does not mean to take up all the meeting time. Others are just as afraid to speak up. The guide may not have the skills or confidence to intervene. Other members would be concerned if they knew that the Circle was not permitting me to say what I need to say to get what I need from the Circle.

Circle impact: Because no one is speaking up, I am beginning to feel that the Circle is not as safe as it needs to be to have a candid conversation. As each person decides not to intervene, they are probably losing faith that the group is able to work through these problems. The Circle is thus not able to stay focused or on track. Each person will walk away wondering what went wrong. A few may not look forward to the next meeting. The Circle is out of balance.

As you can see, one individual's decision not to resolve a problem has many implications. The individual is harmed, other members are harmed, and the Circle is harmed. By understanding these implications and weighing them against the fear of speaking up, most members will be more likely to speak up. This example also demonstrates why it is so important for each person to develop communication skills to be able to say what needs to be said.

Clarify expectations to prevent disputes

One of the best ways to deal with problems is to anticipate them and create a way to deal with them if they arise. This involves articulating the expectations of the members and describing how the group will deal with breaches of these expectations. The exercise of clarifying expectations not only creates a common understanding for the group, but can establish a bond of respect. Individuals who participate in creating these guidelines are more apt to understand their importance and are more likely to respect them.

An easy way to clarify expectations is to simply pass

around the talking piece and ask each person to describe a meeting "pet peeve." You might do this at one of the initial meetings. Two major Circle pet peeves are latecomers and running over time. Each person will hear how others are bothered by certain behaviors and can begin to develop some guidelines or a meeting protocol. These guidelines tend to be more meaningful than a pre-set list of rules.

Another option is to brainstorm a list of things that might cause problems. Here is a sample list that might result from such a brainstorm:

- being late for meetings
- not paying attention
- speaking to others during the meeting
- leaving early
- interrupting others
- speaking for too long
- giving advice when not asked
- being disrespectful

After this discussion you may want to write down some of the things that are important to the group. Some Circles prefer to draft a few simple rules and have all the members formally agree to them. Here are a few examples of meeting guidelines:

- Be on time and present at each meeting.
- Be responsible for your own comfort.
- If you are going to be late, call someone.

- Be responsible for expressing your own needs.

- Own your experiences by saying "I," not "we."

- Stay within time limits.

- Express appreciation to the Circle Guide.

You can also set out a process for resolving certain types of issues as they arise. For example, one group adopted a "three strikes you are out" rule for missed meetings. Those who missed three meetings would be asked to leave the Circle. Another Circle adopted a rule requiring that if a person could not attend a meeting, that person had to contact all the other members and reschedule the meeting within one week from the originally scheduled date.

Use the three Fs to resolve conflict

Another way to resolve conflict is using the three Fs method of communicating in conflict.

Each of us have had both good and bad experiences with conflict. We have been attacked for saying what we think, and we have been embraced for sharing how we feel. Regardless of our experiences, we all know intuitively that honesty is the best policy. We know that healthy relationships require good communication. We know that talking about what is wrong and how it can be improved is best in the long run. By being open and honest we not only resolve our differences, but also re-establish lines of communication and enhance relationships. We all know there is a respectful way to express our thoughts. We just need to develop communication skills to reinforce this way.

The most simple and effective way to communicate in conflict is by using what I call the three Fs conflict resolution technique. The Fs stand for facts, feelings and future. When you find yourself in a situation of conflict, just think about the following three questions: What are the facts? What are my feelings? and What do I want to have happen in the future? Here is how you can apply them in a Circle.

Facts. Describe the behavior that you saw using "I" statements. For example, "My sister told me that you spoke to her about my work situation that I mentioned in our last Circle meeting." Stick to the facts and not opinions.

Feelings. Describe how the behavior made you feel or impacted you. Do not blame or jump to conclusions. For example, "I had not told my sister about the situation and it put me in an awkward situation. I felt the principle of confidentiality had been breached."

Future. Describe your needs to allow for this event to be prevented in the future. For example, "I need to know that what I say in the Circle stays in the Circle."

It is useful to write out these three steps and the words you will use. Here are a few more examples of the three Fs in action:

Script: *I noticed that a few speakers are talking more than others. [Fact] This makes me feel that others may not be engaged. [Feeling] Perhaps we can take a break or pass around the talking stick to find out how others feel. [Future]*

Script: *I see that we are having difficulty reaching consensus on our Circle Purpose Statement. [Fact] I feel tired and a bit frustrated. [Feeling] Maybe we need to go away and come back at the next meeting to discuss it. [Future] How do others feel?*

Script: *I noticed that our meetings have been ending at about 6:15 as opposed to 6:00 as we agreed. [Fact] I feel awkward reminding everyone that I have to leave at 6:00 p.m. [Feeling] Can we have a conversation about this so I can have confidence that we will end on time in the future? [Future]*

With a bit of practice, you will begin to use this three-step method in resolving all sorts of differences in your work and other relationships.

Troubleshooting common problems

Although the Circle Process is designed to create a safe place where members can speak candidly, difficult situations will always arise. Here are a few typical situations that arise in Circles, with some ideas about how to solve them.

Loss of focus

Over time it is easy for a Circle to lose focus. This is often reflected in the group becoming too social. Although members may enjoy the social aspects, if you have come together with a common purpose, you must respect the intention of the whole group. If members feel that the group has become too social, they must say so, sooner rather than later.

An easy way to start a conversation is to say something like "I am feeling that we are spending more and more time on socializing. Could we have a conversation about this at this meeting or the next?" Another way to refocus on the conversation is to have the group revisit their original Circle Purpose Statement. This will remind everyone about why they are meeting and what they should be accomplishing during the Circle.

One bad apple

There may be a rare situation when members feel that one person is not contributing to or benefiting from the Circle. If any member is being disruptive to the proper growth of the Circle, it is important to have a candid Circle discussion. Like apples, one bad apple can spoil the whole bunch. If a member is continually late or fails to follow through on a commitment, it can deplete the morale of the group and cause the Circle to lose effectiveness. It also tends to draw energy from the group, since it is on everyone's mind.

Unfortunately this problem tends to emerge slowly and the Circle tends to compensates to such an extent that it might be difficult to clearly identify this as the problem. In these situations it is best not to brush it aside or hope that it will improve. Here is a sample script to use:

> **Script:** *Before we begin the formal discussion, I would just like to have a short conversation. As you all know, it is our own responsibility to raise things that are bothering us in the Circle. I feel a bit uncomfortable mentioning it, but I have noticed that*

George has not been on time for the last few meetings. I know he has provided reasonable explanations each time, but my preference would be to talk about the impact of this on the group. Perhaps we could start by reviewing our ground rules?

One way to begin this conversation is by having the Circle recommit to the Circle Principles and Practices. This will reconfirm the initial agreements that form the foundation of respect and safety required in the Circle. It is also useful to review your Circle Purpose Statement and ask each member to talk about how the Circle is working and not working, in a more general way. If the behavior does not change, a more assertive approach will be needed.

In most situations, if an individual is not benefiting from the Circle, then the Circle is usually not benefiting from that individual. The decision to leave a Circle should be a mutual decision, and only in rare situations would a member be asked to leave.

Members who dominate

There may be a member in your group who talks too much, asks too many questions or dominates the discussion. If one or two people monopolize the conversation, then other members' needs are often not being met. It is fine to have certain people speak more than others, but it is also important to ensure that over time each person has the opportunity to fully participate.

The main way to prevent members from dominating a conversation is to have each person monitor their own participation. This means saying what you have to say and then allowing others to speak. This also means not speaking even when you might feel the need.

The flip side of this is to speak up when you feel that others are taking up too much time. This supports the principle of each member being responsible for their own needs. Here is an example of how to ask for what you need.

> **Script:** *Catherine, I think I can appreciate what you are saying. It sounds like you are really stuck and can't seem to figure out what to do. I would really like to hear from others about their experiences or ideas on the topic.*

Another way to prevent one person from dominating a conversation is to enforce time limits. By allowing each person a set amount of time, monopolizing is less likely to occur. The final way is to ask the Circle Guide to intervene. The guide could say something like this:

> **Script:** *John, I am going to ask you to stop just for a minute. I have noticed others getting distracted, and I was wondering how others are feeling. Perhaps you could tell us specifically what you want from the Circle right now.*

One member who is silent

Although a Circle is designed to allow people to participate or not participate as they wish, if a member does not say anything for two meetings, there is a problem. A continuously silent member can throw the Circle off balance and make it less effective, and such silence can cause a member to feel isolated. Although it is tempting to view this situation as being an individual's personal problem or choice, it is definitely worth a conversation.

There are many reasons for silence. A member may feel unsafe or feel that they are not able to contribute. This can be caused by the lack of an opportunity to speak, lack of comfort or lack of desire. Regardless, it is best to check and make sure there is not something wrong in the Circle that is causing the problem.

There are two ways to deal with a silent member – individually or in the Circle. One member could approach the quiet member and gently inquire by saying something like "I noticed you were quiet today at the meeting" and wait for a response. A similar comment could be made during a Circle meeting. Another option is for the Circle Guide to open a space for the quieter members. For example, the guide could wait until it looks as if the silent member wants to speak, then say something to the whole Circle such as "I just want to take a moment to ensure we are creating a space for every person to speak."

Stagnation

At some point in the Circle, stagnation can occur. This can mean a general loss of interest in the Circle, boredom or simply a lack of meaningful conversations. In a healthy Circle the time will feel like it is flying by. Some say they feel like they are in the flow. Members leave with a sense of contribution and learning. When a Circle is stagnating, the meeting can feel uncomfortable, awkward or a waste of time.

Although each individual member will at some point feel that the Circle is not meeting their expectations, in a healthy Circle this is usually short-lived. If the stagnation is felt by a good number of people and over an extended period of time, this can be a real problem.

The important thing to keep in mind is that stagnation does not usually mean that the Circle is deteriorating. A Circle will go through good times and rocky times. Do not give up too early. It usually means that the Circle is a bit off track or off kilter.

This stagnation can be caused by a host of reasons, such as an inexperienced Circle Guide or an overzealous member. Rather than trying to locate the precise cause, the easiest way to correct this problem is by going back to fundamentals. Have the group revisit the Circle Principles and Practices and their Circle Purpose Statement. If the statement needs refining, do it. This process will likely spark a deeper conversation about how the Circle is working and not working. This is good.

A person reveals too much

Many people feel uncomfortable when others tell them personal information, and some feel it is too much to handle. Topics such as death, suicide, divorce and sexuality can lead Circles into caverns of silence. The most important thing to remember is that the Circle is not a therapy group and that no one should try to fix the "problem."

The simplest way to deal with revelations of a personal nature is to acknowledge the person's feelings and ask what the person wants from the group. For example, you might say, "Kevin, that sounds terrible. It must be very difficult for you. I am glad you could bring it up to the group, but I am at a loss about what to say. How can this Circle help you?" Usually this will be enough to alert the member that others may feel uncomfortable. If not, a more direct approach may be needed, such as using the three Fs technique.

Inviting new members

When your Circle decides to add a member, the group must decide how to select the new member, how to bring the new member up to speed and how to formally bring the person into the Circle.

Adding a new member can place unexpected pressure on a Circle. The Circle will not only be new for the incoming member, but will also feel new for the current members.

> **Real life.** Susan is a member of a Circle that has been together for over five years. Her friend Jana asked to join the Circle. Susan invited her to the upcoming meeting. Susan phoned each of the other members to let them know Jana was coming. At the meeting everyone felt awkward and the conversation was different than usual. Over the next few months there were many private conversations among the other members about Jana and concerns about her "fit." No one discussed the matter in any of the meetings. Within six months two of the original members quit the Circle without providing much of an explanation.

This situation might have been prevented if the group had talked about how to select and introduce the new member. This scenario also highlights the difficulty people have in speaking candidly. This is why the Circle Process is so critical.

By agreeing ahead of time to have a conversation, you support more authentic conversations.

When selecting new members, it is best to talk about it long before a new member is being considered. Decide how a name is to be brought forward and how you will decide on the member. For example, one member could be responsible for speaking to candidates and providing them with information about the Circle Process. This member could then report back to the Circle. Before joining the Circle, a new member might want to speak to a few members to get a better sense of that Circle.

If a member is invited to join a Circle, then another member should provide this member with a bit of background and information about the Circle. At the minimum this would include information about the Circle Principles, Practices and Process, and the Circle Purpose Statement.

When a new member first attends a Circle, time should be designated to the welcoming. At the minimum, the Circle Guide should welcome the new member and allow the new member to speak. It is useful to have each member introduce themselves around the Circle. This can be an opportunity to reintroduce members to each other. Another option is to ask a few members to describe some personal learning from past Circles. At some point the new member will need to adopt the Circle Principles, Practices and Purpose Statement.

Dealing with departures

If one member decides to leave the Circle, it is important to mark the departure and also mark the starting of a new Circle without this person. Often remaining members feel a sense of loss or a sense of responsibility for the departure. Therefore it is useful to have a discussion, preferably with the member present.

It is best to have the person who is leaving participate in a closing Circle. During this Circle each member should have an opportunity to speak either to that person or to the others about their thoughts and feelings. A farewell ritual might consist of each member providing a positive comment to the person leaving. For example, a member could say something like "Len, your sense of humor will be missed." The departing member may want to respond to each comment or after hearing them all.

Some Circles appoint one person to speak to the departing person to find out more about why the person is leaving and how they feel about the departure. This can be useful information for improving the Circle and allowing the members to better understand the person's reasoning.

If the departing member is absent for their last meeting, the group should dedicate time and perhaps a ritual to recognize the contributions of that member and to recognize that all Circles have beginnings and endings. The departure must be respected by the Circle.

Evaluating your Circle

You will want to periodically evaluate your Circle to determine how well it is working. This can be done informally or formally. An informal evaluation might consist of a general conversation about what is working and what could be improved. Here are some questions you might want to use in this type of discussion:

- What do you enjoy most about this Circle?

- How have you benefited most from this Circle?

- How could participation be encouraged?

- What has been most difficult for you in the Circle?

- How effective is the Circle at resolving differences?

- How well does the Circle Guide role work?

- How does the Circle encourage or discourage commitment?

- What parts of the Circle process could be improved?

- What would you like to focus on next year?

A more formal evaluation is one in which the specific parts and results of the Circle are measured, usually by a written questionnaire. A questionnaire could be developed and provided to members to complete between meetings. It can then be used as a basis for discussion. It should never be used for tabulating data while outside the Circle. Evaluation, like other issues, must be part of a conversation.

The benefit of such an evaluation is that members are able to pinpoint specific areas for improvement. A formal evaluation can evaluate the process or the results. The following is a list of the things you might like to measure in a process-based evaluation and in a results-based evaluation. It is best to use these lists as a starting point for developing your own evaluation questionnaire. Focus on the things that you see as most important to your Circle.

Process-based evaluation

Ask members to describe how they feel about each part of the Circle Process, namely:

Logistics

- Location
- Time
- Members
- Selection of members

One Circle Principles

- Equality
- Confidentiality
- Commitment
- Shared ownership
- Shared leadership

One Circle Practices

- Intention
- Speaking
- Listening
- Guiding

The One Circle Process

- Preparing for the Circle
- The Opening
- The Check-In

- Topic Selection
- The Conversation
- The Check-Out
- The Closing

Circle Purpose Statement

Meeting ground rules

The Circle Guide

- Selecting the Circle Guide
- The effectiveness of the guide
- Rotated or permanent

The Circle Conversation

- Participation
- Satisfaction
- Sufficient time
- Relevant topics

Circle relationships

- Commitment
- Support
- Respect
- Cohesion
- Trust
- Conflict resolution

Results-based evaluation

For a results-based evaluation you measure results. In the preface of this book I suggested that a person who is part of a Circle will benefit by being able to do the following:

- create solutions and solve problems

- gain wise advice and information

- generate contacts and resources

- develop skills and continuously learn

- achieve goals and balance

- obtain support and connection

You may want to take this list and expand it to include the specific results that your Circle has provided. In practical terms, this means constructing a survey asking members the extent to which they have achieved the desired results from their time in the Circle. Here are some sample questions. As a result of the Circle have you:

- received useful advice?

- found solutions to difficult problems?

- expanded your support network?

- been more focused?

- become more effective?

- achieved more balance in your life?

- achieved goals more quickly?

- grown your business or practice?

- reignited your interest in work or business?
- advanced more quickly in your profession or career?
- received challenge and support from the Circle?
- solved problems more effectively?
- made better decisions?
- increased personal or professional effectiveness?
- learned about books or other resources?
- enhanced your skills?
- increased your confidence?
- obtained names of contacts or leads?
- other? _____

As stated at the start of this chapter, even the best-run Circle can run into problems periodically. By dealing with these problems promptly and respectfully, the group can avoid fracturing and ending without proper closure.

....

Chapter 9

The Future
of Circles

It is not because things are difficult that we do not dare; it is because we do not dare that things are difficult.   —Seneca

If we have no peace it is because we have forgotten that we belong to each other.

—Mother Teresa

There is the risk you cannot afford to take, [and] there is the risk you cannot afford not to take.

—Peter Drucker

Being in Circles will impact us in more ways than we can imagine. In Circles we listen, we speak, we learn and we connect. But perhaps more importantly, we change. As described by Pranis, Stuart and Wedge in *Peacemaking Circles:*

> Circles provide the space in which we reveal ourselves, uncover our core humanity, and allow others to feel, know, and touch us. We can't walk through the sacred space of Circles and emerge as we were. We're deepened, and from those depths, we find the power to create our worlds anew – together.[1]

I believe that the One Circle model and other circle processes will impact individuals, families, communities and the world. People who sit in circles can't help but begin to treat each other better. Through meaningful conversations, they develop empathy and necessarily become more tolerant and accepting of others and their differences.

As we sit in Circles we reinforce the fact that we are all connected and that we share the same fundamental human needs. We take this learning to our jobs and begin to change corporate cultures and how we treat each other at work. We apply our Circle learning in our homes and undoubtedly improve our relations with family and friends. This is the just the beginning of the potential ripple impact of Circles.

As I look at the increasing numbers of people using Circles today, I can't help but wonder why they were lost for so long, particularly given their strong historic roots. However, I believe that the time is ripe to bring Circles back. The overemphasis on the individual and the lack of emphasis on the community in our society is causing harm. I agree with Whybrow, Garfield and others who suggest that the current emphasis on individualism has become a liability and that people won't find happiness all alone. I believe that meaning is found in social bonds and intimacy.

My hope is that the One Circle model will eventually be used by people all over the world, not just to create a personal advisory board but to resolve conflict, build trusting teams and create a new way of being together. As described by Christina Baldwin in her book *Calling the Circle*:

> The Circle is an organizational structure that locates leadership around the rim and provides an inclusive means for consulting, delegating tasks, acknowledging the importance of people, and honoring the spiritual. Circle is a useful structure for learning, governing, creating community, providing services, envisioning and stating long range goals.[2]

I share the dream of Christina Baldwin that Circles will become part of the mainstream culture. When this happens we will look back on our traditional ways of communication as basic and awkward. Courageous conversations will abound and differences will be encouraged.

Because the principles of Circles involve so much common sense and are easy to adopt, I have no doubt that Circles will find many uses. I urge you to find your own uses and to continue to explore Circles in everything you do.

Notes

PREFACE
1. Andrews, 1998, 206–7.

CHAPTER 1
1. Garfield, Spring & Cahill, 1998, 35.
2. Whybrow, 2005, 229.
3. Engel, 2000, 23.

CHAPTER 2
1. Bolen, 1999.
2. Starhawk, 1997, 115.
3. Andrews, 1998, 221.
4. Starhawk, 1997, 100–101.

CHAPTER 3
1. Starhawk, 1997, 99.

CHAPTER 4
1. Andrews, 1998, 223.
2. Graveline, 1998, 141.
3. Andrews, 1998, 223–24.
4. Engel, 2000, 189–90.
5. Garfield, Spring & Cahill, 1998, 143.
6. Carnes & Craig, 1998, 174–78.

Chapter 5
1. Engel, 2000, 191.
2. Zimmerman & Coyle, 1996, 18.
3. Ibid., 20.
4. Ibid., 28.
5. Pranis quoted in Engel, 2000, 206.
6. Zimmerman & Coyle, 1996, 22.
7. Carnes & Craig, 1998, 97.
8. Engel, 2000, 103.

Chapter 8
1. Zimmerman & Coyle, 1996, 48.

Chapter 9
1. Pranis, Stuart & Wedge, 2003, 244.
2. Baldwin, 1998, 38.

References

Andrews, Cecile. 1998. *The Circle of Simplicity: Return to the Good Life.* New York: HarperCollins.

Baldwin, Christina. 1998. *Calling the Circle: The First and Future Culture.* New York: Bantam Doubleday Dell.

Bolen, Jean Shinoda. 1999. *The Millionth Circle: How to Change Ourselves and the World—The Essential Guide to Women's Circles.* Berkeley, Calif.: Conari Press.

Boyes-Watson, Carolyn. 2001. "Healing the Wounds of Street Violence: Peacemaking Circles and Community Youth Development." *CYD Journal,* Community Youth Development 2 (4, Fall): 16–21.

———. 2002. *Holding the Space: The Journey of Circles at* ROCA. Boston: The Center for Restorative Justice, Suffolk University.

Cahill, Sedonia, and Joshua Halpern. 1990. *The Ceremonial Circle: Practice, Ritual and Renewal for Personal and Community Healing.* San Francisco: Harper.

Carnes, Robin Deen, and Sally Craig. 1998. *Sacred Circles: A Guide to Creating Your Own Women's Spirituality Group.* San Francisco: Harper.

Duerk, Judith. 1989. *Circle of Stones: Woman's Journey to Herself.* San Diego, Calif.: Innisfree Press.

Engel, Beverly. 2000. *Women Circling the Earth: A Guide to Fostering Community, Healing and Empowerment.* Deerfield Beach, Fla.: Health Communications.

Garfield, Charles A., Cindy Spring, and Sedonia Cahill. 1998. *Wisdom Circles: A Guide to Self-Discovery and Community Building in Small Groups.* New York: Hyperion.

Graveline, Fyre Jean. 1998. *Circle Works: Transforming Eurocentric Consciousness.* Black Point, N.S.: Fernwood Publishing.

Isaacs, William. 1999. *Dialogue and the Art of Thinking Together: A Pioneering Approach to Communicating in Business and in Life.* New York: Doubleday Currency.

Kauth, Bill. 1992. *Circle of Men: The Original Manual for Men's Support Groups.* New York: St. Martin's Press.

Lane, Robert E. 2001. *The Loss of Happiness in Market Democracies.* New Haven & London: Yale University Press.

Marquart, Michael J. 2004. *Optimizing the Power of Action Learning.* Palo Alto, Calif.: Davies Black Publishing.

Peck, M. Scott. 1987. *The Different Drum: Community Making and Peace.* New York: Simon & Schuster.

Pranis, Kay, Barry Stuart, and Mark Wedge. 2003. *Peacemaking Circles: From Crime to Community.* St. Paul, Minn.: Living Justice Press.

Putnam, Robert, D. 2000. *Bowling Alone: The Collapse and Revival of American Community.* New York: Simon & Schuster.

Remen, Rachel Naomi. 1996. *Kitchen Table Wisdom: Stories That Heal.* New York: Berkley Publishing Group.

———. 2001. *My Grandfather's Blessings: Stories of Strength, Refuge, and Belonging.* New York: Riverhead.

Richardson, Cheryl. 1998. *Take Time for Your Life: A Personal Coach's Seven-Step Program for Creating the Life You Want.* New York: Broadway Books.

Sheehy, Gail. 1995. *New Passages: Mapping Your Life across Time.* New York: Random House.

Sher, Barbara. 1979. *Wishcraft: How to Get What You Really Want.* New York: Viking Press.

———, and Annie Gottlieb. 1989. *Teamworks!* New York: Time Warner.

Starhawk. 1997. *Dreaming the Dark: Magic, Sex and Politics.* Boston: Beacon Press.

Wheatley, Margaret J. 2002. *Turning to One Another: Simple Conversations to Restore Hope to the Future.* San Francisco: Berrett-Koehler.

Whitney, Diana, and Amanda Trosten-Bloom. 2003. *The Power of Appreciative Enquiry: A Practical Guide to Positive Change.* San Francisco: Berrett-Koehler.

Whybrow, Peter C. 2005. *American Mania: When More Is Not Enough.* New York: W.W. Norton.

Zimmerman, Jack, in collaboration with Virginia Coyle. 1996. *The Way of Council.* Las Vegas, Nev.: Bramble Books.

About the Author

Maureen Fitzgerald, PhD, is a lawyer, mediator, author and recognized conflict and collaboration expert. She is the founder and president of CenterPoint Conflict and Collaboration Inc., a company dedicated to helping organizations and groups transform conflict and build resilient teams through writing, training, speaking and facilitating.

Maureen has a bachelor of law (LLB) and a master of laws degree (LLM) from the London School of Economics, specializing in alternative dispute resolution. She also has a commerce degree (BComm) with distinction from the University of Alberta.

Maureen is the author of many articles and several books, including these titles:

- *Corporate Circles: Transforming Conflict and Building Trusting Teams*
- *Hiring, Managing and Keeping the Best,* with Monica Beauregard
- *Mission Possible: Creating a Mission for Work and Life*
- *So You Think You Need a Lawyer: How to Screen, Hire, Manage or Fire a Lawyer*
- *Legal Problem Solving: Reasoning, Research and Writing*

As a law professor, Maureen wrote a law school textbook that is now in its third edition and is used in most Canadian law faculties. She has held many leadership positions and volunteer appointments.

Maureen is an international speaker and has appeared on TV news, talk TV and national radio. She mixes humor with practical insights. Through her ability to see things from different perspectives, Maureen challenges others to question their own assumptions. She leaves audiences energized and with an enhanced sense of commitment.

As a master of dialogue, Maureen spends most of her time facilitating conversations – not just to resolve conflict but, more importantly, to build strong relationships. She has become known as "the circle woman" and has a personal mission to take the circle process to the world.

To find out more

Go to www.CenterPointInc.com. You will learn how to do the following:

- book Maureen as a speaker
- sign up for a seminar (live or teleclass)
- create a customized seminar for your group
- purchase bulk copies of this book (discount)
- create customized books or booklets for your group
- obtain a license to provide Circle training

To contact the author

CenterPoint Conflict & Collaboration Inc.
PO Box 72030
Vancouver, BC
Canada V6R 4P2
Ph: 604-228-8900   Fax: 604-228-8909
Email: maureen@CenterPointInc.com
Website: www.CenterPointInc.com

Generic Use and Intellectual Property

The use of circles is growing in many ways and forms, and all uses of circles are encouraged. Maureen Fitzgerald coined the phrase "One Circle" to reflect the process and principles described in this book, which emerged from a combination of years of learning and personal experiences. It is a specific contribution to the growing body of knowledge and specifically includes:

- the five One Circle Principles
- the four One Circle Practices
- the seven-step One Circle Process
- scripts for the first six meetings

Feel free to use any parts of this book. It is hoped that others will build on this model and that Circles will sprout up in many different forms in many different locations.

When using the words "One Circle" or the concepts in this book, please acknowledge the author and the title of this book and refer to CenterPoint Conflict & Collaboration Inc. (www.CenterPointInc.com). Thank you.